the
mediterranean
collection

hamlyn

Editor: Cara Frost
Copy Editor: Anne Crane

Creative Director: Keith Martin
Designer: Claire Harvey

Photographer: Ian Wallace
Food Stylist: Louise Pickford
Stylist: Antonia Gaunt
Indexer: Pamela Le Gassick

Production Controller: Lisa Moore

The Mediterranean Collection
Louise Pickford

First published in 2000 by Hamlyn a division of Octopus Publishing
Group Ltd., 2–4 Heron Quays, London E14 4JP

This edition published 2001

Copyright © 2000 Octopus Publishing Group Ltd.

Distributed in the United States and Canada by
Sterling Publishing Co., Inc.
387 Park Avenue South, New York, NY 10016-8810

British Library Cataloguing-in-Publication Data
A catalogue record for this book is available from the British Library

ISBN 0 600 60391 1

Printed in China

Notes:
Both metric and imperial measures have been given in all recipes. Use one
set of measurements only and not a mixture of both.

Standard level spoon measurements are used in all recipes:
1 tablespoon = one 15 ml spoon
1 teaspoon = one 5 ml spoon

Eggs should be large unless otherwise stated.

Milk should be full fat unless otherwise stated.

Pepper should be freshly ground black unless otherwise stated.

Fresh herbs should be used unless otherwise stated. If unavailable, use
dried herbs as an alternative but halve the given quantities.

Nuts and nut derivatives. This book includes dishes made with nuts and
nut derivatives. It is advisable for customers with known allergic reactions
to nuts and nut derivatives and those who may be potentially vulnerable to
these allergies, such as pregnant and nursing mothers, invalids, the elderly,
babies and children, to avoid dishes made with nuts and nut oils. It is also
prudent to check the labels of pre-prepared ingredients for the possible
inclusion of nut derivatives.

Ovens should be preheated to the specified temperature – if using a fan
assisted oven, follow the manufacturer's instructions for adjusting the time
and temperature.

Louise Pickford

photography by Ian Wallace

the mediterranean

collection

contents

introduction

The flavours of Mediterranean food abound with freshness, colour and vitality – words that could just as easily be used to describe the character of its people. It is of course the people and their lifestyles that have over the centuries shaped the way that the food is cultivated, harvested and cooked today. All the countries bordering the Mediterranean share rich histories of colonization, trade and invasion – turbulent times that have left their mark on everyday life.

It is said that the olive tree heralds the boundaries between the Mediterranean and the rest of Europe and North Africa. Geographically the countries that share the beautiful coastline begin in the west with Spain. To the south lie the exotic countries of Morocco, Algeria, Tunisia, Libya and Egypt. To the east Israel, the Lebanon, Syria and Turkey and finally, to the north, Greece, Italy and southern France, and the various islands that dot the azure blue waters.

We may have become accustomed to the intoxicating ambience of the Mediterranean, but the peace that we see today is a recent development, as the history of these countries is scarred with periods of war and occupation. Today many different cultures and religions sit in relative harmony, sharing much in common and enjoying a similar climate, landscape and coastline. They have a common love of the sea, they are passionate about local herbs, spices and vegetables and yet, despite these similarities, each country has retained its culinary individuality.

The sea itself is probably the most important factor in the way the area has developed over the centuries. The people crossed and recrossed the Mediterranean from early times, to trade and establish colonies, and religious, cultural and culinary influences followed.

The story began several centuries BC with the Phoenicians, from the eastern Mediterranean, who are thought to have been the first people who ever sailed out of sight of land. They established ports and trading posts along the Mediterranean coast and introduced many foods into western Europe, including the pomegranate. By the sixth century BC the Etruscans, from what is now Tuscany, were cultivating vines and then a century later the Greeks, an enthusiastic colonizing nation, came from the north; they planted more vines and cultivated the olive tree.

The spread of the Roman empire began around the second century AD and they too left a heritage that can still be seen today, planting poplars, elms and olive trees. Their cooking methods had a lasting impact as well, with the use of outdoor ovens and the introduction of pastes and sauces.

The next important era was in the seventh century, with the expansion of the Byzantine empire from its capital, Constantinople. These people were merchants and traders and it was their enjoyment of sharing wine and food that epitomizes the whole culture of Mediterranean cuisine that remains today.

After a series of attacks, the Byzantine empire was finally overthrown in 1453 by the Turks, who in turn created the powerful Ottoman empire. Turkey had for centuries provided a major trading post between the Far East and western Europe and through it came exotic foods from as far away as Mongolia and China as well as the Arab world.

Until this time most of the influences had come from the east; however, in the fifteenth century, the Spanish, under the Italian Columbus, reached the Americas, from where they returned with exotic new foods, among them tomatoes, peppers, maize, pumpkins, chocolate, vanilla and of course the potato.

As the Spanish continued their travels west to the New World the culinary tide began to turn and, after the fall of the Ottoman Empire, France, Spain and Italy in turn colonized parts of North Africa and the Middle East. So we see that over a period of about 2500 years countries traded and colonized, invaded and re-invaded neighbouring lands, assimilating and adapting their customs and culture. It is remarkable that any of these nations retained their individuality at all yet we know today that despite similarities in dishes, the dishes differ not only from one country to the next but regionally as well. It is this variety that makes the food of the Mediterranean so vibrant, interesting and, most important of all, so totally enchanting.

The land

The countries of the Mediterranean share a common climate, with searing summers and mild winters interrupted by sudden and violent storms. But the agriculture of a country is determined by its landscape as well as its climate. What to us is a picturesque ideal is also a life of continual struggle and hardship to the people who farm the land, to produce enough food to sustain them during the winter months.

The landscape tends to be one of arid land and rugged mountains, limiting grazing to sheep and goats, which provide meat as well as milk and cheese. Beef is found in parts of Italy, Spain and southern France and occasionally in Turkey and Greece but it is rare in the other countries. Chickens are a domesticated fowl and most families keep them, and game is popular everywhere.

Wheat and maize are grown on the plains, providing most of the staples although rice is grown in several parts of Spain, France and Italy. It is the quality and abundance of vegetables that many of us associate with the Mediterranean diet and a huge quantity and variety of fruits and vegetables are grown in the lush valleys, where the water from the heavy but sporadic rains are collected.

Olive trees thrive in the Mediterranean climate for they love poor, rocky soil, where other crops fail. The mountainous regions of France, Spain, Italy and Greece provide ideal growing conditions and it is the oil produced from the olive that provides the majority of the cooking fat consumed. The origin and exact date for the cultivation of the first olive trees are unknown, but they are recorded in the Middle East and Crete as long ago as 3000 BC, and their spread into the heart of the Mediterranean region was brought about by the ancient Greeks and the Romans.

With an insight into the cultural and geographical history of the area, we come some way towards understanding how the development of the cooking methods and ingredients evolved. But there is another important factor to consider. Mediterranean society is very family orientated, the land is cultivated in smallholdings, families tend to stay together and recipes get passed down through generations. Even today, in a rapidly changing world, many of the women remain at home to cook and, although it can at times be a struggle to produce the food, it is never a chore to prepare. It is this that really characterizes both the Mediterranean people and their cuisine, producing a unique appeal which, despite such a turbulent history, remains today for us all to enjoy.

The food

The Mediterranean cuisine is one of the most colourful and vibrant in the world, providing sensual dishes flavoured with wild herbs gathered from the hillsides; lamb and chicken are often roasted whole over coals; vegetables are abundant and used in a wide variety of soups, bakes and salads. Each country has a favourite staple food – the Italians have their pasta, the Spanish short-grain rice, the Turks bulgar wheat and the Moroccans couscous. Meals are less structured than our own and often small tidbits are eaten throughout the day as people gather in markets or bars to pass the time.

In recent years the Mediterranean diet has received much acclaim for its beneficial health properties. The main fat consumed is olive oil, which is thought to reduce the amount of cholesterol in the body. Butter is rare although it is found in northern Italy, Spain and France but elsewhere it is limited as there are few cows. Milk, yogurt and cheese are produced mainly from sheep's and goat's milk.

Eggs are common and appear in similar but slightly different forms in different countries, in dishes such as the Spanish tortilla, Italian frittata and French omelettes. Egg yolks were first used as long ago as the thirteenth century by the Catalans to thicken sauces like aïoli, the garlic mayonnaise. Similarly, the Greeks and Turks favour egg yolks as a thickening agent and are famous for their egg and lemon sauces that accompany meat and poultry.

Nuts are widely used both to flavour and thicken sauces and are also added to many dishes, from soups and stews to desserts.

Spices were introduced from the east and are particularly prevalent in North African and Spanish cooking, where similarities can be seen. As with all ingredients there is a certain crossover, but whereas saffron is favoured in cooking by the Spanish and North Africans, it is not used a great deal in Greek and Turkish dishes.

Herbs, more than any other ingredient are associated with the cooking of the Mediterranean and are used with abandon. They are added with flair and vigour to almost every dish, creating a wonderful fragrance and sensuality. The herbs most commonly used are basil, coriander, dried and fresh oregano, flat leaf parsley, sage, thyme and rosemary.

Game is popular in France, Italy and Spain. Although some is domesticated much is hunted with great enthusiasm and passion. Game animals include hare, rabbit and wild boar.

The Mediterranean itself is a prime source of sustenance and all the regions that border the sea have an unrivalled passion for its bounty. Fish and seafood are plentiful. If you take a trip to the local harbour in the early morning the sight of the fishermen bringing in their morning catch is a visual feast. Piles of prawns and squid, baskets of red mullet and bass, and barrels of sardines are ready to be taken to the local markets. One of my fondest memories is dining *al fresco* along beachfronts, enjoying the sunset and eating simple, but delicious dishes of grilled squid, octopus and prawns.

Fruit is often added to savoury dishes and, along with nuts, the use of dried fruits is particularly North African in origin. Fresh fruit when eaten as a dessert is usually of one variety and is generally sliced and served chilled. Other desserts are often very sweet, such as the rich nutty baclavas of Greece and Turkey. The Italians are famous for their wide range of ice creams and sorbets whilst the Spanish love custards and pastries.

Despite the obvious similarities in the food and customs of the Mediterranean people it is actually the differences that give each country its culinary individuality. If we look at pasta as an example, we immediately think of Italy and yet pasta is also cooked in Spain where, unlike the Italians who prefer their pasta *al dente* or just done, the Spanish cook it until it is soft and creamy.

The book

I fell in love with the cooking of the Mediterranean many years ago. There is a simplicity combined with an unparalleled passion that has produced dishes that are full of flavour and vitality. Due to the climate and landscape there are periods of feasting and then times of fasting and this sums up perfectly the lifestyle of the Mediterranean people. The seasons are respected, so that foods are cherished and eaten fresh and the glut is preserved for times when food is scarce. Supermarkets exist of course, as they do everywhere, but it is the local markets overflowing with fresh ingredients that epitomizes the character of the area.

Dishes are flamboyant yet conservative. I love the whole way that food is enjoyed; the gathering of friends to share a table of little snacks or a meal that lasts many hours. A simple meal of freshly grilled fish served with a piquant nutty sauce followed by a simple leaf salad allows the flavours of each ingredient to shine through. What I wanted to achieve with this book is not just another collection of old favourites (although some of those are included) but to create new dishes based on the flavours of the various Mediterranean cuisines. In a similar way to the history of the region I am influenced by individual cultures, customs and lifestyles brought together as one glorious celebration of eating.

The ingredients

The basis of all Mediterranean cooking is the use of fresh ingredients, and I cannot emphasize strongly enough the importance of this in everyday cooking. Only use seasonal foods, which will mean that some of these recipes are limited to certain times of the year, but it is far better to choose a different recipe than to cook a dish that will ultimately be disappointing. Finding the best quality ingredients is part of the cooking process, so hunt out top quality suppliers and buy the best food possible.

glossary

Aïoli
Whether it is called *aïoli*, *allioli* or garlic mayonnaise, it is a good rule when making this sauce to use a mild French extra virgin olive oil. Stronger flavoured oils can make the sauce taste bitter.

Anchovies
Small, delicate fish, fresh anchovies are rarely seen outside the Mediterranean. Salted anchovies, which are then dried or canned, are widely available. Dried anchovies have a better flavour and texture. Wash off the salt and remove the backbone before using them. They may need soaking in milk for 30 minutes to remove excess saltiness.

Bouquet garni
This is a small collection of herbs, spices or aromatics tied together in muslin and used to flavour stews and soups. You can buy them from specialist food stores, but it is far better to make your own. The contents vary but a good selection would include a short length of celery, a bay leaf, sprigs of parsley and thyme, a peeled garlic clove and a few peppercorns. Lemon and orange peel, spices and other herbs can also be added depending on the dish.

Bulgar wheat
Sometimes called cracked wheat, this is a grain made from hulled wheat that is boiled until it cracks. It needs to be rehydrated in boiling water to swell and soften the grains before use. Bulgar wheat is one of the staple foods of Greece, Turkey and Middle Eastern countries.

Capers
The caper shrub grows throughout the Mediterranean. The full, but unopened buds are picked and salted or preserved in brine or oil. Rinse thoroughly before use.

Cheese
Feta is a Greek and Turkish sheep's milk cheese traditionally stored in a salty whey or brine. It has a crumbly texture and milky white appearance and is mainly used in salads, or as a filling for savoury pastries.
Haloumi is a Turkish slightly salty, semi-hard sheep's milk cheese used in cooking. It is sliced and fried or grilled and must be eaten immediately after it is cooked or it becomes rubbery.
Kasar is a hard sheep's milk cheese available in Turkish food stores. Use pecorino sardo as an alternative.
Kefalotyri is a Greek cheese made from sheep's milk. It is a hard cheese with a slightly salty flavour, ideal for grating. Parmesan or pecorino sardo may be used as substitutes.
Mascarpone is an Italian soft cream cheese made from cow's milk, from the Lombardy region. It is eaten fresh or added to cakes and pastries.
Mozzarella, the Italian cheese traditionally made from buffalo's milk, is a wonderfully soft, creamy cheese that should be eaten raw in a salad or simply drizzled with olive oil. The slightly inferior cow's milk mozzarella is better for cooking, for pizzas, lasagne and pies.
Parmesan is the hard, cow's milk cheese from Italy used as an accompaniment to pasta and risottos. Buy Parmigiano Reggiano in a piece and and keep it wrapped in waxed paper in the refrigerator, grating it as and when needed.
Pecorino is the Italian generic name for all sheep's milk cheeses. Pecorino romano and sardo are the best-known varieties. It is a hard cheese similar to Parmesan, ideal for grating, with a mildly nutty flavour.
Ricotta is an Italian fresh cheese made from the whey left after making other types of cheese. The Italians also salt ricotta for use in savoury dishes, but this is rarely available outside Italy. Use fresh ricotta in pasta stuffings and cakes or eat it with a sprinkling of sugar and cinnamon.

Chickpea flour
Also called gram flour, this is made from ground chickpeas. It is used mainly in Indian cookery, but is also found in Provençal and North African cooking.

Chillies
There are many varieties of chillies found in Mediterranean cooking, with the hottest being used in North African dishes. Deseed chillies for a milder flavour and add them sparingly at first. Dried chilli flakes are especially fiery as they include the seeds as well as the flesh. Always wash your hands after handling chillies and do not touch your eyes.

Couscous
The staple dish of North African cooking, this is a semolina grain that is ground, dampened and then rolled in fine flour to coat it, expanding its size. Couscous is traditionally cooked slowly over a stew, so that the steam moistens the grains and adds flavour. Most brands of couscous have been pre-cooked, so always check the instructions on the packet.

Fennel
The bulb is used as a vegetable, the stalks and feathery fronds (leaves) as a herb and the tiny seeds as a spice, making this aniseed-flavoured vegetable particularly versatile. The stalks of the fennel plant are often dried out and then thrown on to hot barbecue coals to add flavour to the food cooking above them.

Fideus
Small lengths of very thin pasta used in Catalan dishes, especially those with seafood. You can buy fideus from Spanish delicatessens or substitute thin Italian pasta like capellini, and break it into 5 cm (2 inch) lengths. The Spanish cook pasta until it is soft, rather than *al dente* like the Italians.

Filo pastry
Sometimes spelled phyllo, these paper-thin pastry sheets are used for savoury pastries and pies in Greek, Turkish, Middle Eastern and North African cuisines. The sheets dry out quickly, so keep them covered with a damp tea towel. Filo pastry is available in various sizes; 28 x 45 cm (11 x 18 inch) sheets are probably the most useful.

Globe artichoke
This stunning vegetable is actually a member of the thistle family and the centre contains a choke that must be scooped out. Freshness is vital for a good flavour so choose large, bright green artichokes with no brown spots. The flesh browns on exposure to air, so have a lemon at hand to rub on the cut surfaces.

Ham
There are several types of raw, cured hams mentioned in this book, including Parma from Italy, Bayonne from France and Serrano from Spain. You can use any one of these depending on availability.

Harissa
This Moroccan spice paste is traditionally stirred into a *tagine* (stew) to add flavour and bite. It is made from rehydrated and ground chillies and packs a powerful punch, so add with caution.

Herbs
Integral to Mediterranean cooking, herbs are used in abundance. There are many different types and those used most frequently include basil, coriander, dill, marjoram, mint, oregano, flat leaf parsley, rosemary, sage and thyme. Buy fresh herbs in bunches whenever possible, as they are far better value for money. Store in plastic bags in the refrigerator, with a spray of water on them, where they should last for several days. Oregano is unusual in that the dried herb is used more frequently than the fresh.

Lemons
Use unwaxed lemons, especially for sliced and grated rind, if possible.

Olives
The olive tree produces a stone fruit which is either harvested and pressed to make oil or left to ripen for eating. Olives vary in colour from green to brown through to purplish black; these are just stages of ripeness. The best olives for eating include:
Kalamata, a Greek olive which is a pointed oval, pale brownish-black olive with a slightly acidic taste.
Niçoise olives are tiny, pale brown olives with a sweet, firm flesh.
Tuscan olives are a glossy black, with a wrinkled flesh and earthy flavour.

Olive oil
This is an essential ingredient in Mediterranean cooking and plays an important part in the diet of today's health-conscious society, for it is a fat that actually reduces the cholesterol in the body and also tastes fantastic. There are different qualities of olive oil depending on the level of acidity:
Extra virgin is made from the first cold pressing of fresh olives and is the highest quality oil, generally from a single estate. It has a maximum acidity of one per cent and the finest flavour. It is the most expensive olive oil and is best used drizzled on to bread or over salads.
Virgin olive oil is the next best quality and is often made from cold-pressed oils from different estates. The maximum acidity is two per cent. It has a less distinctive flavour than extra virgin and is less expensive.
Pure olive oil is almost certainly refined. From a third or fourth pressing, it is likely to have been heat-treated, which destroys the unique character of the oil.

The character, colour and flavour of olive oil varies not only from country to country but also from region to region. Generally speaking, Italian oil is deep green with a peppery taste, while Spanish oils are more yellow in colour with a mellow flavour. Greek oils are dense and green with a strong olive taste. France produces less oil which tends to be mild in flavour.

Orange flower water
Used in North African and Middle Eastern cooking to flavour syrups, pastries, desserts and salads, it adds an exotic, slightly perfumed flavour.

Orzo
A tiny rice-shaped pasta used in Italian and Greek cooking.

Pancetta
This is an Italian bacon with a slightly sweet flavour. It is available both smoked and unsmoked, in a piece or sliced, from Italian delicatessens. It seems to have less water content than streaky bacon and a superior flavour, but bacon can be substituted.

Pasta
This is an Italian staple food. Dried pasta, made with durum wheat, is suitable for most dishes. Commercially available fresh pasta is generally poor, with a floury taste and chewy texture. Dried egg pasta is usually excellent.

Pine nuts
These are the small pointed fruits of the stone pine, indigenous to the western Mediterranean. Sometimes called pine kernels, they have a soft, oily texture and are used in the classic Italian sauce, pesto.

Polenta
An Italian staple, polenta is fine maize flour or cornmeal. Most brands are now instant, so follow individual cooking instructions.

Pomegranate syrup
A thick, dark syrup extracted from sour pomegranates, it is widely used in North African and Middle Eastern cooking. It has a sharp, sweet flavour.

Porcini
This is the Italian name for the wild mushroom known in Britain as cep. It grows in deciduous woods. Dried porcini are also available.

Preserved Lemons
A Moroccan lemon pickle with a sharp flavour and creamy texture, added to meat and fish stews.

Pumpkin
The best-known member of the squash family, the pumpkin is found in many dishes throughout the Mediterranean. Italians are especially fond of it for stuffed pasta dishes. Squashes can be used instead of pumpkin in most recipes.

Quince
This beautiful fruit is a member of the apple and pear family and tastes a little like both. It has a pale, wax-like skin with hard, cream-coloured flesh. It cannot be eaten raw, due to its high pectin level and is often made into jams, jellies and pastes. It is popular all over the region and is added to meat dishes, as well as to fruit desserts.

Rice
Risotto rice is an Italian rice that is able to absorb a great deal of the cooking liquid without becoming soft. This is what gives the dish, risotto, its characteristic creamy texture. Arborio and carnoroli are extremely fine risotto rices and, although expensive, they are worth looking for. The Spanish version is Valencian rice, used in paella and other rice dishes. It is not so creamy as its Italian counterpart and may be difficult to obtain.

Rocket
A peppery salad herb, known as *roquette* in France and *arugula* in Italy.

Salt cod
Dried and salted cod is very popular in Spain, Portugal and southern France. It is available from specialist food stores and some fishmongers. Look for thick pieces of fish with plenty of flesh. It keeps well, wrapped in clingfilm in the refrigerator, for several months. Soak in water for 24 hours before using.

Sausages
Chorizo is the Spanish, red sausage flavoured with paprika and garlic. There are two main types, the softer, less cured sausage must be cooked before eating whereas the dried cured chorizo is sliced and eaten as a *tapa*. *Italian* sausages vary from region to region. A particular favourite is the *luganega* from northern Italy. It is spiced with garlic and pepper. Use a good pork sausage with herbs and spices as a substitute. *Toulouse* sausages are made from coarsely chopped pork similar to a good quality British cooking sausage.

Seafood
Clams are popular throughout the Mediterranean, usually one of the small varieties, such as Venus clams. The tiny ones, called *vongole* in Italy, are only 2.5–5 cm (1–2 inches) across. They are available from good quality fishmongers. Scrub thoroughly before cooking and discard any that do not open when cooked.
Crab meat is available vacuum-packed from good fishmongers, but fork through to remove any pieces of shell or cartilage. It is also available frozen from supermarkets.
Mussels are especially popular in southern France and Spain. Mediterranean varieties usually have dark blue-black shells, but the large Spanish mussels are a mottled brown. Scrub well under cold water and pull off the beards. Discard any that do not open when sharply tapped with a knife and any that remain shut after cooking.
Prawns Choose fresh, cooked or raw prawns if possible, with their heads and shells intact. Frozen raw prawns are nearly as good. Always remove the black vein that runs along the prawn's back before cooking.

Semolina
This is ground durum wheat, which is used to make pasta. Semolina is slightly more granular than flour, pale yellow in colour and with a high gluten content.

Spices
Allspice is a member of the pepper family and, as the name implies, is a spice with several flavours. Good with both sweet and savoury dishes.
Juniper berries are the small, purple-black berries used to flavour gin. When lightly crushed, they release a pine-like aroma.
Paprika is sold as sweet, hot or smoked and is the dried and ground flesh of the *capsicum annuum,* a type of pepper. Hot paprika is not actually hot, but has a deep flavour. The Spanish use paprika to flavour sausages, sauces and fish dishes.
Saffron strands are the extracted red or yellow stigmas of the purple crocus, which is mainly produced in La Mancha in Spain. Buy the strands, avoiding the inferior powder. Saffron is the world's most expensive spice, but only a little is required.
Star anise is most commonly associated with eastern cooking, but like most spices it has travelled far and wide.

Squid ink
Small sachets of squid ink are available from good fishmongers. It is used to flavour rice dishes.

Sun-dried tomatoes
Buy tomatoes stored in olive oil, drain and use as required. Sun-dried tomato paste is sold in tubes and jars, or make your own by processing the tomatoes in a little of their oil.

Tahini
A paste made from grinding toasted sesame seeds, it is used mainly in Turkey and the Middle East to add flavour to sauces and is an essential ingredient in hummus.

Tomatoes
Really ripe vine tomatoes are recommended for the recipes in this book, as they are the closest to those that are used throughout the Mediterranean. They have a far better flavour than tomatoes picked when green and left to ripen. Look for tomatoes with bright red, firm flesh and a viny smell.

Trahana
A Greek pasta made with flour, semolina or bulgar wheat, and sour milk. It is used to add flavour and texture to soups and stews.

Vinegars
Balsamic vinegar from Modena in northern Italy, is dark, mellow and sweet. It is matured in wooden barrels for up to 20 years. It is quite expensive, but a little goes a long way. *Sherry vinegar* is the Spanish equivalent of balsamic, with a rich flavour. Buy from a reliable source, as some cheap brands taste bitter.

Vine leaves
These are usually available in brine or vacuum packs. Wash the leaves well before use.

Vanilla pods
These are the dried, cured seed cases of an orchid plant that are used to add a hint of vanilla to creams and custards. Once you have used the pods you will not want to go back to using vanilla essence.

Warka
Moroccan pastry, similar to filo, but slightly thicker and less delicate. It is used to make *bisteeya*, the savoury chicken pie.

Yeast
Dry active yeast comes in granular form and must be dissolved in warm water before it can be added to flour. *Fast acting yeast* or easy-blend yeast, is sold in sachets and can be mixed directly into the flour.

little dishes

The custom of serving a selection of savoury snacks is popular all round the Mediterranean. They are known as *tapas* in Spain, *antipasto* in Italy and *mezze* in Greece, Turkey and the Middle East. Although traditionally a variety of dishes is set out for people to dip into, the dishes in this chapter are designed to be served as a starter, if preferred.

salt cod fritters with beetroot hummus

greece

750 g (1½ lb) salt cod (to give you 8 good fish finger-sized pieces of fish)

a little milk

vegetable oil, for deep-frying

Beetroot hummus:

25 g (1 oz) day-old bread (without crusts)

200 g (7 oz) cooked beetroot, chopped

1 tablespoon tahini

1 garlic clove, crushed

½ teaspoon ground cumin

50–75 ml (2–3 fl oz) extra virgin olive oil

1–2 tablespoons lemon juice, to taste

salt and pepper

Batter:

1 egg, separated

1 tablespoon olive oil

100 ml (3½ fl oz) light beer

65 g (2½ oz) plain flour, plus extra for dusting

To garnish:

lemon wedges

flat leaf parsley sprigs

A recipe inspired by a wonderful dish served at a local Greek restaurant in London – these crispy coated salt cod fingers are complemented perfectly by the slight sweetness of the beetroot hummus. Start the process of soaking the cod the day before you wish to serve it.

1 Place the cod in a bowl and cover with plenty of cold water. Leave to soak for 24 hours, changing the water several times if you can. Wash the cod again under cold water.

2 Using a sharp knife, skin and fillet the cod as you would a piece of fresh fish and pull out any small bones with a pair of tweezers. Cut the fish into fingers and soak in milk for 2 hours. Dry thoroughly on kitchen paper.

3 To make the hummus, process the bread in a food processor to make crumbs, then add the beetroot, tahini, garlic and cumin and process until fairly smooth. Gradually blend in enough oil to make a thick sauce, then season to taste with lemon juice and salt and pepper. The consistency should resemble classic hummus.

4 To make the batter, put the egg yolk, oil, beer, flour and salt and pepper into a large bowl and beat until smooth. Cover and set aside for 30 minutes, then whisk the egg white and fold it in.

5 Heat 5 cm (2 inches) of vegetable oil in a deep pan to 180°C (350°F) or until a cube of bread browns in 30 seconds. Dust the cod fingers lightly with flour, then dip them into the batter and fry for 2–3 minutes, until crisp and golden. Drain well and keep warm in a low oven while frying the rest. Serve hot with the beetroot hummus and garnished with lemon wedges and parsley sprigs.

Serves 4

Variation: Fresh cod can be used instead of salt cold. Skin and fillet 500 g (1 lb) cod and cut it into fingers. Sprinkle with salt and set aside for 1 hour. Wash and dry well, then continue as above.

crab briks with aïoli

tunisia

Tunisian in origin, a brik is a small savoury pastry made with warka, a pastry similar to filo, with a variety of different fillings. Traditionally a brik always contains beaten eggs as well as meat, fish or vegetables.

25 g (1 oz) butter

1 shallot, finely chopped

1 garlic clove, crushed

1 red chilli, deseeded and chopped

2 eggs, lightly beaten

squeeze of lemon juice

pinch of paprika

250 g (8 oz) fresh white crab meat

4 large sheets of filo pastry (each about 28 x 45 cm/11 x 18 inches)

egg white, for brushing

vegetable oil, for deep-frying

salt and pepper

Aïoli (see page 134), to serve

1 Melt the butter in a small frying pan and gently fry the shallot, garlic and chilli for 5 minutes until softened but not browned. Stir in the egg, lemon juice and paprika and stir over a low heat until the mixture is dry.

2 Remove from the heat, set aside to cool, then stir in the crab meat and season with salt and pepper to taste.

3 Take a sheet of pastry (keeping the remaining sheets covered with a slightly damp, clean tea towel) and fold crossways into three. Brush the surface with a little egg white and place a quarter of the crab mixture at one end. Fold the pastry over once, then fold the ends over, brushing them with a little egg white as necessary. Continue to roll the pastry over to form 'pillows', pressing the edges together to seal. Repeat to make 4 briks.

4 Heat 5 cm (2 inches) of vegetable oil in a deep pan to 180°C (350°F) or until a cube of bread browns in 30 seconds. Fry 2 briks at a time for 4–5 minutes until they are golden and crisp. Keep warm in a low oven while frying the remaining 2 briks. Serve the crab briks hot, with the alioli.

Serves 4

baba ganoush

turkey

This spiced aubergine pâté comes in many guises, with each recipe varying slightly. Some include tahini, others yogurt, but this version with the slightly unusual addition of chopped mint is my particular favourite.

1 Prick the aubergines all over with a fork and put them into a preheated oven, 200°C (400°F), Gas Mark 6, for 20–30 minutes, until the skins wrinkle and the flesh feels collapsed, turning them halfway through cooking. Set aside to cool.

2 Slice open the aubergines and scrape the flesh into a food processor, adding all the remaining ingredients except the oil and seasoning. Process to form a fairly smooth paste and then gradually blend in the oil to soften the texture. Season with salt and pepper to taste and serve with griddle bread or pitta.

Serves 6

2 aubergines

1 garlic clove, crushed

½ teaspoon ground cumin

1 tablespoon tahini

2 tablespoons chopped mint

1 tomato skinned, deseeded and diced

4–6 tablespoons extra virgin olive oil

salt and pepper

Griddle Bread (see page 112) or pitta, to serve

cheese fritters

cyprus

Kefalotyri is a Greek hard sheep's milk cheese which can be found in Greek shops, but pecorino sardo or Parmesan can be used instead. If wished, these small cheese fritters can be made ahead of time and reheated in a moderate oven for about 10 minutes.

1 Place all the ingredients in a bowl and stir together to form a sticky batter.

2 Heat 5 cm (2 inches) of vegetable oil in a deep pan to 180°C (350°F) or until a cube of bread browns in 30 seconds, then using a tablespoon, carefully slip spoonfuls of the cheese mixture, 4 at a time, into the oil. Fry for 2–3 minutes, turning halfway through, until crisp and golden. Drain on kitchen paper and keep warm in a low oven while frying the remaining fritters.

3 Serve the fritters as hot as possible with lemon wedges for squeezing over.

Serves 4–6

50 g (2 oz) haloumi cheese, diced

50 g (2 oz) feta cheese, crumbled

25 g (1 oz) Kefalotyri cheese, grated

25 g (1 oz) plain flour

1 egg, beaten

1 tablespoon milk

½ tablespoon chopped coriander

½ tablespoon chopped mint

¼ teaspoon ground cumin

pinch of ground cinnamon

pepper

vegetable oil, for deep-frying

lemon wedges, to serve

chorizo with broad beans

spain

250 g (8 oz) shelled broad beans
125 g (4 oz) spicy chorizo sausage
1 tablespoon olive oil
2 garlic cloves, roughly chopped
1 tablespoon chopped dill
1 tablespoon chopped mint
juice of ½ lemon
salt and pepper
crusty bread, to serve

Tapas bars serve this dish, or different versions of it, all over Spain, although actually I first tasted it in England, served by a Spanish friend.

1 Blanch the beans in lightly salted boiling water for 1 minute, then drain and refresh under cold water. Dry well.

2 Cut the sausage into slices about 5 mm (¼ inch) thick. Heat the oil in a frying pan, add the garlic and fry gently for 2–3 minutes, until softened, then discard. Increase the heat, add the sliced chorizo and stir-fry for 2–3 minutes, until it is golden and has released some of its oil.

3 Stir in the beans and cook for a further 2–3 minutes, then add the herbs, squeeze over the lemon juice and season to taste with salt and pepper. Serve warm with crusty bread.

Serves 4–6

summer vegetables with herb aïoli

france

The beauty of this dish will be obvious to those lucky enough to grow their own vegetables. For the rest of us, memories of Mediterranean markets abundant with summer vegetables picked only hours before must suffice. It's worth sourcing the vegetables for this dish from a local farm shop or good quality greengrocer.

1 To make the aïoli, crush the garlic cloves with the sea salt in a mortar or by pounding them together on a board with the side of a knife blade. Place in a food processor with the egg yolks, lemon juice, mustard and pepper and process briefly until pale.

2 With the motor running, gradually pour in the oil through the feeder funnel in a steady stream until the sauce is emulsified, thick and glossy. Add the herbs towards the end, to give a lovely bright green, mottled effect. You may need to thin the aïoli slightly by whisking in a spoonful or two of boiling water.

3 Check over the vegetables, wash away any dirt and pat dry. Arrange the vegetables on a large platter and serve with lemon wedges and the herb aïoli.

Serves 4

500 g (1 lb) fresh summer vegetables

lemon wedges, to serve

Herb aïoli:

2–8 garlic cloves, depending on personal taste

½ teaspoon sea salt

2 egg yolks

1 tablespoon lemon juice

1 teaspoon Dijon mustard

300 ml (½ pint) French extra virgin olive oil (see page 8)

4 tablespoons mixed herbs, to include basil, chives and parsley

1–2 tablespoons boiling water (optional)

pepper

radishes with provençal butters

france

Although one associates the south of France with olive oil, butter is used in many dishes and is often flavoured with locally grown herbs and aromatics. You will find small pots of differently flavoured butters to eat with bread on restaurant tables.

For each butter:

50 g (2 oz) butter, at room temperature

1–2 teaspoons olive oil

Saffron flavouring:

½ teaspoon saffron threads

pinch of sea salt

Basil and garlic flavouring:

15 g (½ oz) basil leaves

1 garlic clove, crushed

squeeze of lemon juice

salt and pepper

Anchoïade flavouring:

25 g (1 oz) pitted black olives, chopped

2 salted anchovy fillets, drained and chopped

pepper

To serve:

young radishes

sliced French sticks

sea salt and pepper

1 To make the saffron butter, first grind the saffron threads with the sea salt to make a powder, then purée with the butter and olive oil.

2 To make the basil and garlic butter and the anchoïade butter, simply combine all the ingredients in a food processor and process until smooth.

3 Roll each butter into a log then wrap in clingfilm. Chill until required, then serve with the radishes, sliced French sticks and sea salt and pepper.

Serves 12

tuna carpaccio with crisp capers

italy

50 g (2 oz) salted capers, rinsed
1 tablespoon plain flour
3 tablespoons olive oil
125 g (4 oz) tuna fillet
25 g (1 oz) pecorino sardo cheese
a few salad leaves

Dressing:
½ small shallot, finely chopped
1 teaspoon lemon juice
½ teaspoon Dijon mustard
¼ teaspoon sugar
6 tablespoons extra virgin olive oil
salt and pepper

Wafer-thin slices of melt-in-the-mouth tuna are topped with fried capers with an unusual mustardy lemon dressing.

1 Dry the capers on kitchen paper and dust with the flour. Heat the oil in a small frying pan and fry the floured capers for 2–3 minutes until crisp and golden. Drain thoroughly on kitchen paper.

2 To make the dressing, place all the ingredients in a bowl and whisk well until combined.

3 Using a sharp knife, cut the tuna into wafer-thin slices, cutting down across the grain. Arrange on serving plates, top with the capers, some shavings of pecorino and a few salad leaves. Drizzle with the dressing and serve immediately.

Serves 4

spanish tortilla

spain

There are many recipes for tortilla, the classic Spanish omelette, but I have often been disappointed with the results. They just never taste as good as those I've enjoyed in tapas bars, but recently I've discovered that the only way to make an authentic tortilla is to use quite indecent quantities of olive oil. However, don't let this put you off; some of the oil is drained away before the tortilla is cooked and, after all, a little Spanish omelette goes a very long way.

1 Heat the oil in a large frying pan, add the potatoes, onion and a little salt and fry over a low heat for about 20 minutes, stirring occasionally to prevent sticking and browning.

2 Beat the eggs in a large bowl. Lift the potatoes and onions out of the pan with a slotted spoon and stir them into the beaten eggs, adding a little more salt and some pepper. Set aside to soak for 10 minutes. Pour off the oil, reserving 3 tablespoons.

3 Return 2 tablespoons of the oil to the pan and heat until hot. Add the potato mixture, reduce the heat and cook gently for for about 10 minutes, until it is golden underneath and almost set. Carefully flip the tortilla on to a large plate so the cooked side is on top. Add the remaining oil to the pan, ease the tortilla back in, and cook the second side for about 5 minutes.

4 Remove the tortilla from the frying pan. Serve warm or leave to cool, cut into squares or wedges.

Serves 10–12

200 ml (7 fl oz) extra virgin olive oil
750 g (1½ lb) waxy potatoes, cubed
1 onion, chopped
4 large eggs
salt and pepper

pamboli amb tomatiga

majorca

Literally translated pamboli *means bread with oil. It is eaten as an appetizer all over the island of Majorca, in much the same way as the Italians eat bruschetta. The Majorcans rub their toasted bread with a particular kind of tomato which is sold in bunches. They have tough skins making them perfect for squeezing. I substitute very ripe vine tomatoes for their flavour, but squeezing them is slightly messy.*

1 Griddle or grill the bread until well toasted and rub all over with the garlic, if using. Take a tomato half and rub over one side of the toast, squeezing as you go to extract the pulp and seeds. Drizzle the toast liberally with oil and add a little vinegar, salt and pepper. Eat immediately.

Serves 2

Variation: For a more opulent topping, add slices of cured ham, olives and capers.

2 slices of country bread
1 garlic clove, peeled but left whole (optional)
1 tomato, halved
extra virgin olive oil
red wine vinegar
salt and pepper

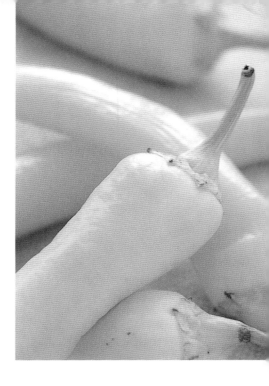

fried peppers with feta

turkey

If you've visited Turkey or a Turkish market, you will probably have spotted the wide range of peppers that are sold there, including the slightly curly pale green variety, about 12–15 cm (5–6 inches) long, that looks disarmingly like an anaemic chilli. Well fear not; this is a pepper and tastes mild and sweet and is perfect for this snack.

1 Cut the peppers in half lengthways and carefully extract the seeds. Place the peppers on a baking sheet, rub them all over with a little oil and grill for 2–3 minutes on each side, until charred and softened.

2 Transfer the peppers to a serving platter and top them with the garlic, feta and parsley. Drizzle over plenty of oil, a little vinegar or lemon juice and season generously with salt and pepper. Serve warm.

Serves 4

8 pale green Turkish peppers

extra virgin olive oil

1 garlic clove, sliced

125 g (4 oz) feta cheese, cut into slices

1 tablespoon chopped parsley

red wine vinegar or lemon juice

salt and pepper

gnocchi parcels
with basil oil

italy

475 g (15 oz) floury potatoes

1 large egg, beaten

1 teaspoon salt

1 tablespoon olive oil

175–185 g (6–6½ oz) plain flour

basil leaves, to garnish

freshly grated Parmesan cheese,
to serve

Filling:

1 tablespoon olive oil

½ garlic clove, crushed

1 small shallot, finely chopped

50 g (2 oz) sun-dried tomatoes in
oil, drained and chopped

150 g (5 oz) ricotta cheese

salt and pepper

Basil oil:

50 g (2 oz) basil leaves

8 tablespoons extra virgin olive oil

pinch of salt

1 Boil the potatoes until really tender; drain well and return to the pan to dry out over a gentle heat. Pass through a potato ricer or mouli, cool slightly and then work in the egg, salt, olive oil and enough flour to make a soft dough. Knead on a lightly floured surface then shape into a ball. Wrap in clingfilm and leave to rest while preparing the filling.

2 To make the filling, heat the oil in a small saucepan and gently sauté the garlic and shallot until soft but not browned. Purée with the tomatoes, ricotta and salt and pepper to taste.

3 Knead the dough briefly, divide it into six pieces and roll one piece out thinly. Stamp out five 7.5 cm (3 inch) rounds using a pastry cutter and dampen the edges with a little water. Place a teaspoon of filling in the centre of each round, fold it in half and press the edges together to seal. Repeat to make 30 parcels, place on a floured tray, cover and freeze for at least 2 hours.

4 When you are ready to serve, bring a large saucepan of lightly salted water to a rolling boil. Meanwhile make the basil oil. Pour boiling water over the basil leaves so they just wilt, refresh them under cold water and dry thoroughly. Purée the leaves with the oil and a little salt, to make a vibrant green sauce.

5 Plunge the frozen gnocchi into the pan of boiling water, return to the boil and cook for 5–6 minutes, then drain well. Serve with a little basil oil and some freshly grated Parmesan cheese and garnish with basil leaves.

Serves 6

soups & stews

Mediterranean soups are generally the chunky variety – hearty wholesome dishes, full of deep earthy flavours, rather than the more smooth, sophisticated veloutés of northern Europe. Pulses and grains are widely used in soups and stews, which are often highly spiced. Traditionally many would have been cooked in deep earthenware pots, such as a Moroccan *tagine,* but they are easily adapted to the modern saucepan.

tomato & bread soup

italy

After an eventful journey to a small trattoria outside Florence and negotiating the menu with very little Italian between us, I finally ordered this classic bread and tomato soup. It was served at room temperature and was so dense you could cut it with a knife. The flavours were simply fantastic and I have tried to replicate it on many occasions. This hot version comes pretty close to the original. It can also be served at room temperature if wished.

1 kg (2 lb) really ripe vine tomatoes, skinned, deseeded and chopped

300 ml (½ pint) vegetable stock

6 tablespoons extra virgin olive oil

2 garlic cloves, crushed

1 teaspoon sugar

2 tablespoons chopped basil

100 g (3½ oz) day-old bread, without crusts

1 tablespoon balsamic vinegar

salt and pepper

Pesto (see page 138), to serve (optional)

1 Place the tomatoes in a saucepan with the stock, 2 tablespoons of the oil, the garlic, sugar and basil and bring gradually to the boil. Cover the pan and simmer gently for 30 minutes.

2 Crumble the bread into the soup and stir over a low heat until it has thickened. Stir in the vinegar and the remaining oil and season with salt and pepper to taste. Serve immediately or leave to cool to room temperature. Stir a spoonful of pesto into each bowl before serving, if liked.

Serves 4

walnut soup

turkey

4 tablespoons walnut or olive oil

1 onion, finely chopped

1 garlic clove, crushed

1 teaspoon ground cinnamon

¼ teaspoon each ground cumin and coriander

175 g (6 oz) walnuts, toasted and chopped

50 g (2 oz) dried breadcrumbs

1 litre (1¾ pints) vegetable stock, or Chicken Stock (see page 139)

1 tablespoon lemon juice

1 tablespoon pomegranate syrup

salt and pepper

To serve:

Greek yogurt

chilli oil

An intense, rich soup made with toasted and ground walnuts that can be found all over the Middle East and also in North Africa, where nuts are widely used in cooking.

1 Heat the oil in a saucepan and fry the onion, garlic, cinnamon, cumin and coriander for 5 minutes, until lightly golden. Add the walnuts and breadcrumbs and fry gently for a further 5 minutes, stirring occasionally.

2 Transfer the spice mixture to a food processor, add a spoonful of the stock, the lemon juice, pomegranate syrup and salt and pepper. Process to form a paste, then gradually blend in the remaining stock.

3 Return the soup to the saucepan and bring slowly to the boil. Cover and simmer for 15 minutes, then season with salt and pepper to taste. Serve topped with a spoonful of Greek yogurt and a drizzle of chilli oil.

Serves 6

bean & cabbage soup

spain

175 g (6 oz) dried broad beans, soaked overnight in cold water

250 g (8 oz) chorizo sausage for cooking (see page 9)

2 rosemary sprigs

bouquet garni

1.7 litres (3 pints) cold water

2 tablespoons olive oil

1 onion, chopped

2 garlic cloves, crushed

1 small red pepper, cored, deseeded and chopped

pinch of cayenne pepper

250 g (8 oz) Savoy cabbage, shredded

1 tablespoon chopped parsley

salt and pepper

To serve:

olive oil

crusty bread

1 Drain and rinse the soaked beans and put them into a saucepan with 125 g (4 oz) of the chorizo in a piece, the rosemary, bouquet garni and cold water. Bring to the boil and boil rapidly for 10 minutes, then simmer gently, covered, for 1–1½ hours, until the beans are tender.

2 Heat the oil in a frying pan and fry the onion, garlic, red pepper and cayenne for 5 minutes. Dice the remaining chorizo, add to the pan and fry for a further 5 minutes.

3 Stir the onion mixture into the cooked beans with the cabbage and salt and pepper. Bring to the boil and cook for 20 minutes. Add the parsley, adjust the seasoning and spoon into warmed bowls. Drizzle with olive oil and serve immediately with crusty bread.

Serves 4

pumpkin soup with coriander pistou

france

Coriander is used in the pistou *(the French word for pesto), replacing the more familiar basil, and adding a North African influence to this Provençal soup.*

1 Place the pumpkin, thyme sprigs and garlic cloves in a roasting tin to fit in snugly in a single layer. Add half of the oil and toss gently to coat well. Season liberally with salt and pepper and roast in a preheated oven, 200°C (400°F), Gas Mark 6, for 30 minutes, until charred and softened.

2 Meanwhile, heat the remaining oil in a deep saucepan and gently fry the onion, celery and chilli for 10 minutes, until softened. Add the stock, bring to the boil and simmer, covered, for 20 minutes. Stir in the roasted pumpkin and all the pan scrapings, then return to the boil and simmer for 5 minutes.

3 Discard the thyme sprigs, then transfer the soup to a food processor or blender and purée, in batches, until really smooth. Keep warm.

4 Place all the ingredients for the coriander pistou in a spice grinder and grind to form a smooth paste, or use a pestle and mortar. Spoon the soup into warmed bowls and swirl a little pistou into each one.

Serves 6

500 g (1 lb) pumpkin flesh, cubed

4 thyme sprigs

4 garlic cloves, peeled but left whole

4 tablespoons olive oil

1 onion, chopped

2 celery sticks, sliced

1 red chilli, deseeded and chopped

1.2 litres (2 pints) vegetable stock

salt and pepper

Coriander pistou:

25 g (1 oz) coriander leaves

1 garlic clove, crushed

1 tablespoon blanched almonds, chopped

4 tablespoons extra virgin olive oil

1 tablespoon freshly grated Parmesan cheese

salt and pepper

harira

morocco

1.5 kg (3 lb) free-range chicken

2–4 tablespoons olive oil

1 onion, chopped

4 garlic cloves, crushed

1 teaspoon grated fresh root ginger

2 teaspoons hot paprika

¼ teaspoon saffron threads

2 x 400 g (13 oz) cans chopped tomatoes

900 ml (1½ pints) water

125 g (4 oz) cooked chickpeas (from a can)

50 g (2 oz) red lentils

50 g (2 oz) basmati rice

juice of 1 lemon

2 tablespoons each chopped parsley and coriander

1–2 tablespoons Harissa (see below), optional

salt and pepper

grilled pitta bread, to serve

Harira is the soup eaten during the holy month of Ramadan in Muslim countries throughout North Africa and the Middle East. Made with lamb or chicken and flavoured with pepper, lemon and tomatoes, the soup would traditionally have been thickened with yeast or flour. I find the soup tastes even better the next day when it thickens naturally, as the liquid is absorbed by the rice and lentils.

1 Joint the chicken into eight pieces (or ask your butcher to do this for you). Heat the oil in a saucepan and brown the chicken pieces on all sides. Remove with a slotted spoon.

2 Add more oil to the pan, if necessary, then add the onion, garlic and ginger and fry gently for 10 minutes, until lightly golden. Return the chicken to the pan and add all the remaining ingredients except the herbs and harissa, if using. Cover and simmer gently for 45 minutes.

3 Pick out the chicken pieces, leave them to cool slightly, then gently pull the flesh away from the bones and return it to the soup. Leave the soup to cool completely, then cover and chill overnight.

4 Reheat the soup, stir in the parsley and coriander and harissa, if using, and serve with grilled pitta bread.

Serves 8

harissa

morocco

50 g (2 oz) dried red chillies

2 garlic cloves, crushed

½ teaspoon sea salt

4–5 tablespoons extra virgin olive oil

This is a very fiery chilli sauce from Morocco. If preferred, deseed the chillies before using. Harissa is traditionally added to meat and fish stews, soups and salads, but add it gradually as it is a very hot sauce.

1 Cover the chillies with boiling water and soak for 1 hour.

2 Drain the chillies, pat dry and place in a spice grinder with the garlic and salt. Grind until fairly smooth and then blend in the oil to form a smooth paste.

3 Transfer the harissa to a screw-top jar, cover the surface with a layer of oil and store for up to 1 week.

Makes 100 ml (3½ fl oz)

avgolemono

greece

This is lemon and egg soup that is made throughout Greece. The eggs thicken the soup as it is heated but you must take care when adding them not to boil the soup, as it will curdle.

1 Put the chicken, carrots, onion, celery, bay leaves, peppercorns and water into a saucepan and bring slowly to the boil, skimming the surface to remove any scum. Lower the heat and simmer gently for 30 minutes.

2 Strain the stock into a clean pan and carefully strip the chicken into bite-sized pieces. Add the rice to the stock and simmer until cooked.

3 In a small bowl, beat together the egg yolks, lemon juice and 2 tablespoons of the stock, then gradually whisk this back into the rest of the stock. Add the chicken, parsley and salt and pepper and warm through without boiling. Serve hot.

Serves 4

2 chicken quarters, each about 375 g (12 oz)

2 carrots, chopped

1 small onion, sliced

1 celery stick

2 bay leaves

6 white peppercorns

900 ml (1½ pints) water

50 g (2 oz) long-grain rice

2 egg yolks

3 tablespoons lemon juice

4 tablespoons chopped parsley

salt and pepper

gazpacho & almond soup

spain

Gazpacho is the classic cold tomato and vegetable soup of Spain, with as many different recipes and versions as there are towns. I like this particular recipe, which is thickened with almonds, although dried or fresh breadcrumbs can be used instead. Reserve some of the diced vegetables to garnish.

1 Place the tomatoes, onion, garlic, peppers, cucumber, chillies, olives and capers in a food processor or blender and purée until fairly smooth, then thicken the soup by blending in the almonds.

2 Transfer the soup to a bowl and stir in the vinegar, sugar, cold stock, tomato juice and olive oil. Cover and chill in the refrigerator for at least 1 hour, then stir in the herbs. Season with salt and pepper to taste and serve garnished with some extra diced vegetables and toasted flaked almonds.

Serves 6–8

1 kg (2 lb) really ripe vine tomatoes, skinned, deseeded and diced

1 small red onion, chopped

4 garlic cloves

2 green or red peppers, cored, deseeded and chopped

½ cucumber, peeled and chopped

2 red chillies, deseeded and chopped

25 g (1 oz) pitted green olives, chopped

1 tablespoon salted capers, rinsed

50 g (2 oz) ground almonds, toasted

3 tablespoons red wine vinegar

1 tablespoon sugar

450 ml (¾ pint) cold vegetable stock

150 ml (¼ pint) tomato juice

150 ml (¼ pint) extra virgin olive oil

2 tablespoons each chopped coriander and parsley

salt and pepper

To garnish:

a few extra diced vegetables

toasted flaked almonds

spiced chickpea &
lamb soup

turkey

The great thing about this richly spiced soup is the ease with which it is prepared and cooked. All the ingredients are put straight into a casserole (traditionally an earthenware dish) and baked until tender.

1 Drain the soaked peas and beans, wash them well and drain again. Place them in separate pans, cover with plenty of cold water and bring to the boil. Simmer for 1 hour, drain and reserve the liquid.

2 Place the cooked pulses in a clay pot or casserole dish, add all the remaining ingredients and cover with the reserved liquid, adding extra water to cover, if necessary.

3 Cover the casserole with a tight-fitting lid and bake in a preheated oven, 180°F (350°F), Gas Mark 4, for 1½ hours, until the meat and vegetables are tender.

4 Serve each bowl of soup drizzled with olive oil and pass around some crusty bread.

Serves 6

50 g (2 oz) chickpeas, soaked overnight in cold water

50 g (2 oz) black-eyed beans, soaked overnight in cold water

50 g (2 oz) trahana or bulgar wheat

500 g (1 lb) neck of lamb, cut into 4

4 tablespoons olive oil

1 onion, chopped

2 carrots, chopped

400 g (13 oz) can chopped tomatoes

4 small red chillies

4 thyme sprigs

1 teaspoon each ground coriander cumin and cinnamon

½ teaspoon each dried mint and oregano

salt and pepper

To serve:

olive oil

crusty bread

seafood soup

spain

Many Spanish dishes can be identified by the presence of nuts, used to flavour and thicken sauces. The seafood in this recipe can be varied to suit individual tastes, perhaps substituting langoustines for the lobsters, or cod for the monkfish.

1 Soak the saffron threads in the boiling fish stock for 10 minutes. While they are soaking, heat half of the oil in a large flameproof casserole and fry the onion, garlic, thyme and chilli flakes for 10 minutes, until lightly golden. Pour in the sherry and boil rapidly until reduced by half, then add the tomatoes, the saffron-infused stock and a little salt and pepper. Bring to the boil and simmer, covered, for 20 minutes. Transfer 150 ml (¼ pint) of the broth to a bowl and reserve.

2 To prepare the seafood, discard the lobster heads, cut the bodies in half lengthways and separate the claws. Cut the monkfish into cubes and dust lightly with flour. Wash and devein the prawns. Scrub the mussels and clams. Add all the seafood to the casserole and return to the boil, stirring well. Cover and simmer for a further 10 minutes, or until all the seafood is cooked.

3 Combine the ground almonds, vinegar, the remaining oil and reserved broth and stir them into the stew, then heat through for 5 minutes until thickened. Serve with crusty bread and accompanied by finger bowls.

Serves 4–6

a few saffron threads

150 ml (¼ pint) boiling Fish Stock (see page 139)

4 tablespoons olive oil

1 onion, chopped

2 garlic cloves, crushed

1 tablespoon chopped thyme

¼ teaspoon dried chilli flakes

100 ml (3½ fl oz) dry sherry

400 g (13 oz) can chopped tomatoes

2 small cooked lobsters, each about 475 g (15 oz)

500 g (1 lb) monkfish fillet

2 tablespoons plain flour

12 large raw prawns, peeled

500 g (1 lb) fresh mussels

500 g (1 lb) fresh clams

50 g (2 oz) ground toasted almonds

1 tablespoon sherry vinegar

salt and pepper

crusty bread, to serve

provençal fish soup with rouille

france

This is my favourite version of the Provençal fish soup, *bouillabaisse, which is served with rouille, toasted French bread and Parmesan cheese. Traditionally the fish used in Provence always includes wrasse or rascasse, mullet and gurnard; however, any wide selection of fish, such as grey mullet, mackerel and cod, will still give an intensely flavoured soup.*

1 Cut the fish into large chunks, heads and all. Heat half of the oil in a heavy-based frying pan and fry the fish and prawns, in batches, for 5–8 minutes, until browned. Remove with a slotted spoon and transfer to a large flameproof casserole.

2 Add the remaining oil to the frying pan and gently fry the onions, garlic, fennel, thyme and cayenne for 10 minutes, until the onions have softened. Add the brandy and boil rapidly until reduced by half.

3 Scrape the contents of the pan into the casserole and stir in the tomatoes, tomato paste, saffron threads and cold water. Bring to the boil, skim the scum from the surface, then cover and simmer gently for 30 minutes. Remove the casserole from the heat and leave to cool for 30 minutes.

4 Meanwhile, make the rouille. In a food processor, blend together the garlic, chilli, salt and egg yolk until pale, then with the motor running, add the oil through the funnel in a slow, steady stream until the sauce is thickened and glossy. Add 1 tablespoon of the fish broth, blend again, then taste and adjust the seasoning. Transfer to a bowl and cover with clingfilm.

5 Purée the fish soup with all the bits, in batches, until as smooth as possible. Pass through a sieve into a clean pan, rubbing and pressing down hard to extract all the liquid. Return the soup to the heat and simmer gently for 15 minutes, until reduced slightly.

6 Spoon the soup into warmed bowls and top each one with a slice of toasted French bread spread with some rouille and a good sprinkling of Parmesan cheese.

Serves 6

1.25 kg (2½ lb) mixed fish, cleaned and scaled

250 g (8 oz) conger eel steak

250 g (8 oz) raw prawns

4 tablespoons olive oil

2 onions, chopped

2 garlic cloves, crushed

1 fennel bulb, trimmed and diced

1 tablespoon chopped thyme

1 teaspoon cayenne pepper

50 ml (2 fl oz) brandy

2 x 400 g (13 oz) cans chopped tomatoes

2 tablespoons sun-dried tomato paste

large pinch of saffron threads

1.5 litres (2½ pints) cold water

Rouille:

1 garlic clove, crushed

1 dried red chilli, deseeded and chopped

¼ teaspoon salt

1 egg yolk

150 ml (¼ pint) French extra virgin olive oil

To serve:

French bread, sliced and toasted

freshly grated Parmesan cheese

clam, potato & bean stew

spain

2 tablespoons olive oil

125 g (4 oz) piece of unsmoked
pancetta, diced

1 onion, chopped

375 g (12 oz) potatoes, cubed

1 leek, sliced

2 garlic cloves, crushed

1 tablespoon chopped rosemary

2 bay leaves

400 g (13 oz) can cannellini
beans, drained

900 ml (1½ pints) vegetable stock

1 kg (2 lb) small clams or mussels,
scrubbed

salt and pepper

crusty bread, to serve

Garlic and parsley oil:

150 ml (¼ pint) extra virgin olive oil

2 large garlic cloves, sliced

¼ teaspoon salt

1 tablespoon chopped parsley

This soup is Spanish in origin, but I encountered it in a restaurant in Palma, Majorca, and vowed to reinvent it at home. This is my interpretation.

1 Heat the the oil in a large saucepan and fry the pancetta for 5 minutes, until golden. Remove from the pan with a slotted spoon. Add the onion, potatoes, leek, garlic, rosemary and bay leaves to the pan and sauté gently for 10 minutes, until softened. Add the beans and stock, bring to the boil and simmer gently for 20 minutes, until the vegetables are tender.

2 Meanwhile, make the garlic and parsley oil. Heat the oil with the garlic and salt in a small pan and simmer gently for 3 minutes. Leave to cool, then stir in the parsley. Set aside.

3 Transfer half of the soup to a blender and blend until really smooth, then pour it back into the pan and season with salt and pepper to taste. Stir in the clams or mussels and add the pancetta to the soup. Simmer gently until the shellfish are open, about 5 minutes (discard any that remain closed). Spoon the soup into bowls and serve drizzled with the garlic and parsley oil and serve with some crusty bread.

Serves 6

salads & vegetable dishes

It is the abundance of fresh vegetables that epitomizes the Mediterranean diet. They are combined with a natural flair and together with olive oil, garlic, herbs and spices provide a wide variety of wonderful dishes. Artichokes, aubergines and mushrooms are enhanced by fragrant herbs and aromatic spices, salad leaves are tossed with sweet fruits and sharp dressings, and tomatoes are roasted for several hours for their flavours to develop. Serving a selection of vegetable dishes typifies the way food is enjoyed in the Mediterranean.

fatoush salad with fried haloumi

egypt/greece

An Egyptian-Greek inspired salad of diced vegetables tossed with a lemon dressing and topped with fried haloumi cheese. Serve as a starter or a light lunch dish.

1 Combine the peppers, cucumber, tomatoes, onion, garlic and herbs in a large bowl, then whisk together the dressing ingredients and toss with the salad until well coated.

2 Griddle or grill the pitta until toasted, tear it into bite-sized pieces and add to the salad. Stir well and leave to infuse for 20 minutes.

3 Heat the oil in a frying pan and fry the haloumi slices on both sides for 2–3 minutes, until golden and softened. Serve with the salad.

Serves 4

2 green peppers, cored, deseeded and diced

½ cucumber, diced

4 ripe tomatoes, diced

1 red onion, finely chopped

2 garlic cloves, crushed

2 tablespoons chopped parsley

1 tablespoon each chopped mint and coriander

2 pitta breads

4 tablespoons olive oil

125 g (4 oz) haloumi cheese, sliced

lemon dressing:

6 tablespoons extra virgin olive oil

1–2 tablespoons lemon juice

1 tablespoon water

¼ teaspoon sugar

salt and pepper

green bean & potato salad

spain

The distinctive flavour of sherry vinegar gives this dish its identity, but make sure you buy a good quality sherry vinegar from a Spanish delicatessen or specialist food store, as some cheaper brands can taste unpleasant.

500 g (1 lb) new potatoes
500 g (1 lb) green beans
1 white onion, thinly sliced
4 slices of serrano ham

Dressing:
6 tablespoons extra virgin olive oil
2–3 teaspoons sherry vinegar
1 garlic clove, thinly sliced
½ teaspoon ground cumin
pinch of sugar
salt and pepper

To garnish:
2 tablespoons chopped parsley
2 hard-boiled eggs, chopped

1 Bring a large saucepan of lightly salted water to the boil, add the potatoes and cook for 8 minutes, then add the beans and continue to cook for a further 4–5 minutes, until they are both tender. Drain and refresh the vegetables under cold water and pat dry.

2 Combine the beans, potatoes and onion in a large bowl. Whisk all the dressing ingredients together and mix with the vegetables. Arrange the slices of ham over the top and garnish with the parsley and chopped eggs. Serve immediately.

Serves 4

spiced potatoes

tunisia

This is such a tasty way of cooking potatoes; they are fried gently with onions and spices and then braised in chicken stock until tender, absorbing the flavours as they cook. You probably won't need to add salt to this dish, as the salt in the stock intensifies as it reduces. These potatoes are great served with roast chicken or lamb.

1 Cut any large potatoes in half. Heat the oil in a saucepan and fry the onion and garlic for 5 minutes until softened, then add the spices and potatoes and toss well until evenly coated. Cover the pan and fry gently for 5 minutes.

2 Add the stock and bring to the boil, then partially cover the pan and cook over a low heat for 30 minutes, until the potatoes are really tender and the liquid reduced and syrupy. Serve immediately.

Serves 4

500 g (1 lb) new potatoes

2 tablespoons olive oil

1 small onion, finely chopped

1 garlic clove, crushed

1 teaspoon ground turmeric

pinch of saffron threads

½ teaspoon each ground cumin and coriander

300 ml (½ pint) Chicken Stock (see page 139)

slow-roasted tomatoes

italy

Here, the tomatoes are roasted for several hours on a bed of salt, which extracts the water content leaving them shrivelled, lightly caramelized and totally delicious. They have many uses – as a crostini topping, a salad or vegetable accompaniment and they are particularly good with the Butterflied Leg of Lamb with Roasted Garlic on page 84.

1 Make a bed with the sea salt in a shallow roasting dish, just large enough to hold the tomato halves in a single layer. Arrange the tomatoes, cut side up, in the salt and top with the herbs and some pepper.

2 Transfer the dish to a preheated oven, 230°C (450°F), Gas Mark 8, for 20 minutes, then reduce the temperature to 150°C (300°F), Gas Mark 2 and continue to cook for a further 1½ hours, until the tomatoes are shrivelled and fairly dry. Leave to cool on a plate and serve drizzled with plenty of olive oil.

Serves 4

125–175 g (4–6 oz) sea salt

6 really ripe vine tomatoes, halved

thyme, oregano and rosemary sprigs

pepper

extra virgin olive oil, to serve

braised provençal artichokes

france

If you've always been put off cooking artichokes because of the somewhat strenuous, labour-intensive preparation involved, then think again. It's actually far quicker and easier than you think, and artichokes taste fantastic.

1 Fill a large bowl with cold water and squeeze in the juice from half of 1 of the lemons. Snap off most of the stem from the artichokes leaving about 2.5 cm (1 inch), peel away as many of the large tough leaves from around the base as possible and cut off a good 2.5 cm (1 inch) from the top. Rub all over with the second lemon half and put into the bowl of acidulated water.

2 Plunge the artichokes into a large pan of lightly salted boiling water, cover and simmer for about 20 minutes, or until they feel tender. Transfer them to kitchen paper, inverting them to extract excess water, and leave until cool enough to handle.

3 Meanwhile, heat 2 tablespoons of the oil in a frying pan and gently fry the garlic, shallots and thyme for 5 minutes. Add the pancetta, fry until golden and then add the tomato and basil. Remove from the heat.

4 Cut the artichokes in half, scooping out and discarding the hairy chokes from the middle, and arrange, cut side up, in a large ovenproof dish. Spoon the tomato mixture into the hollow middles and over the stems, drizzle over the remaining oil and squeeze over the juice from half of the remaining lemon. Season liberally with salt and pepper. Add the wine to the dish, cover and bake in a preheated oven, 180°C (350°F), Gas Mark 4, for 30 minutes, until really tender.

5 Serve hot or warm, garnished with basil leaves and drizzled with plenty more olive oil, a squeeze of lemon juice and with Parmesan shavings.

Serves 4

2 lemons, halved

4 large globe artichokes

8 tablespoons extra virgin olive oil

2 garlic cloves

2 shallots, finely chopped

1 teaspoon chopped thyme

50 g (2 oz) piece of smoked pancetta, diced

1 large ripe beef tomato, skinned and diced

1 tablespoon chopped basil

2 tablespoons dry white wine

salt and pepper

a little shaved Parmesan, to serve

basil leaves, to garnish

mesclun salad with sautéed chicken livers

france

25 g (1 oz) butter

1 shallot, finely chopped

375 g (12 oz) chicken livers, cleaned and halved

a few shredded marjoram leaves

3 tablespoons brandy

175 g (6 oz) mixed salad leaves

2 tablespoons herbs, to include chives, tarragon and parsley

2–3 tablespoons French Dressing (see page 138)

salt and pepper

Mesclun is the French word used to describe the many wild salad leaves that grow in abundance on the hills of Provence. Rocket, lamb's lettuce and dandelion are often found, but any combination of leaves can be used in this salad, either simply presented with a French dressing or, as in this recipe, with a few sautéed chicken livers.

1 Melt the butter in a small frying pan, add the shallot and sauté gently for 5 minutes, until softened but not browned. Increase the heat and fry the livers for 1–2 minutes on each side, until browned on the outside. Add the marjoram and brandy and boil rapidly until the liquid has evaporated. Remove from the heat and cool slightly.

2 Toss the salad leaves and herbs with 2–3 tablespoons of the dressing and arrange on plates, spoon on the livers, season with salt and pepper and serve immediately.

Serves 4

bulgar wheat salad

turkey

175 g (6 oz) bulgar wheat

1 red onion, finely chopped

2 ripe vine tomatoes, finely chopped

¼ cucumber, diced

1 garlic clove, crushed

1 small red chilli, deseeded and finely chopped

4 tablespoons chopped parsley

2 tablespoons each chopped mint and coriander

juice of ½ lemon

6 tablespoons extra virgin olive oil

salt and pepper

This Turkish salad is often served as part of a mezze spread. I usually make it as part of an informal supper with a selection of cold meats and other salad dishes and bread.

1 Put the bulgar wheat into a bowl and cover with boiling water. Leave to soak for 30 minutes, then drain off the excess water.

2 Stir in all the remaining ingredients and season to taste with salt and pepper. Cover and set aside to infuse for at least 30 minutes, for the flavours to develop.

Serves 4–6

carrot salad

morocco

A spiced sweet-savoury salad typical of the flavours used in Morocco and in cooking from other parts of North Africa. The inclusion of orange flower water adds to the exotic nature of the dish.

1 Using a potato peeler, pare the carrots into thin ribbons and place in a large bowl. Peel and segment the oranges over a small bowl to catch the juices. Add the orange segments, olives and parsley leaves to the carrot ribbons and toss together.

2 Whisk the dressing ingredients into the reserved orange juice. Taste and adjust the seasoning, stir the dressing into the salad and serve immediately.

Serves 4

4 large carrots

2 oranges

125 g (4 oz) black olives, pitted and chopped

50 g (2 oz) flat leaf parsley leaves

Dressing:

2 garlic cloves, crushed

juice of ½ lemon

1 teaspoon clear honey

1 tablespoon orange flower water (optional)

a pinch each of ground cinnamon, cumin and coriander

8 tablespoons extra virgin olive oil

salt and pepper

baked squash with mascarpone & sage

italy

2 small acorn squash, each about 500 g (1 lb)

2 tablespoons olive oil

125 g (4 oz) piece of smoked pancetta, diced

2 garlic cloves, crushed

2 tablespoons chopped sage

175 g (6 oz) mascarpone cheese

4 sun-dried tomatoes in oil, drained and chopped

2 tablespoons freshly grated Parmesan cheese

salt and pepper

To serve:

grilled bread

green salad

Acorn squash is a small, dark green, heart-shaped variety of squash and is perfect for this dish, as one is small enough to serve 2 people. Not strictly an Italian recipe, but certainly inspired by the flavours of that country.

1 Cut the squash in half lengthways and carefully scoop out the seeds. Season the shells lightly with salt and pepper and place, cut side up, in a roasting tin. Drizzle with a little of the the oil and bake in a preheated oven, 200°C (400°F), Gas Mark 6, for 45 minutes.

2 Dry-fry the pancetta for about 5 minutes, until it is golden and has released its fat. Lower the heat, add the remaining oil and gently fry the garlic and sage for a further 4–5 minutes, until the garlic is softened.

3 Remove the squash from the oven and fill the hollows with the bacon mixture. Spoon in the mascarpone and scatter over the sun-dried tomatoes and Parmesan. Return to the oven for 15–20 minutes, until bubbling and golden. Serve with some grilled bread and a crisp green salad.

Serves 4

aubergine parmigiani

italy

2 x 400 g (13 oz) cans chopped tomatoes

2 garlic cloves, crushed

1 teaspoon sugar

2 tablespoons chopped basil

6 tablespoons olive oil

3 aubergines

250 g (8 oz) mozzarella cheese, grated

50 g (2 oz) Parmesan cheese, freshly grated

salt and pepper

A classic Italian vegetable and cheese bake with layers of grilled aubergines, tomato sauce, mozzarella and grated Parmesan. It can be served as a vegetable accompaniment to grilled chicken or lamb, or with pasta as a vegetarian main course.

1 Put the tomatoes, garlic, sugar, basil, 2 tablespoons of the oil and salt and pepper into a saucepan and bring to the boil. Cover the pan and simmer gently for 15 minutes, then remove the lid and simmer for a further 15 minutes, until thickened slightly.

2 Meanwhile, thinly slice the aubergines lengthways. Brush each slice with a little of the remaining oil, season lightly and grill or griddle for 3–4 minutes on each side, until charred and tender.

3 Spoon a quarter of the tomato sauce into an ovenproof dish and add one-third of the aubergines and one-third of the two cheeses. Repeat the layers, finishing with tomato sauce and the cheeses. Bake in a preheated oven, 200°C (400°F), Gas Mark 6, for 35–40 minutes until bubbling and golden.

Serves 4

greens with lemon oil

greece

1 kg (2 lb) mixed salad greens (see right)

4 tablespoons olive oil

1 garlic clove, crushed

juice of ½ small lemon

salt and pepper

In Greece and other eastern Mediterranean countries, wild greens are gathered from the fields and hillsides and used extensively in pies, salads and vegetable dishes. I use a combination of salad leaves, such as spinach, rocket and chard, which gives an equally delicious result and serve this as a vegetable dish with fish, chicken or pork.

1 Wash all the leaves well, discarding the thick stalks from the spinach and chard, if using. Transfer the leaves with the water still on them to a large saucepan. Heat gently, stirring until the leaves are wilted.

2 Strain off as much excess liquid as possible, then return the leaves to the pan and stir in the oil, garlic, lemon juice and salt and pepper to taste. Heat gently for 2–3 minutes, until the greens are tender. Serve immediately.

Serves 4

roast porcini with gremolata

italy

I'll never forget a dish of roast porcini I was served in a small trattoria in Rome. It seemed to me that the simplest of dishes made with the best ingredients are impossible to beat. Mushrooms of all descriptions can be cooked in this way. Gremolata is an Italian garnish of parsley, garlic and lemon rind.

500 g (1 lb) porcini or field mushrooms

6–8 tablespoons extra virgin olive oil, plus extra for serving

2 garlic cloves, chopped

grated rind and juice of ½ lemon

2 tablespoons chopped parsley

salt and pepper

1 Cut the porcini into 5 mm (¼ inch) slices and arrange in the base of a large roasting dish. Drizzle with the olive oil and season generously with salt and pepper. Transfer to a preheated oven, 200°C (400°F), Gas Mark 6, and bake for 10–15 minutes, until softened and golden.

2 To make the gremolata, mix together the garlic, lemon rind and parsley.

3 Transfer the porcini to a serving dish, scatter over the gremolata and and serve drizzled with the lemon juice and some extra virgin olive oil.

Serves 4

sweet & sour courgettes

spain

Sweet and sour dishes can be found throughout the Mediterranean.

3 tablespoons olive oil

500 g (1 lb) courgettes, diced

1 garlic clove, crushed

1 red chilli, deseeded and finely chopped

2 tablespoons raisins

2 tablespoons salted capers, rinsed

1 tablespoon sherry or balsamic vinegar

1 teaspoon sugar

2 tablespoons hazelnuts or blanched almonds, toasted and chopped

2 tablespoons water

salt and pepper

chopped parsley, to garnish

1 Heat the oil in a frying pan and stir-fry the courgettes over a high heat for 3–4 minutes, until golden. Lower the heat, add the garlic, chilli and a good sprinkling of salt and fry gently for a further 2–3 minutes, until the garlic is softened.

2 Add the raisins, capers, vinegar, sugar, hazelnuts, water and pepper to the pan, then cover and simmer for 5 minutes.

3 Taste and adjust the seasoning, garnish with the chopped parsley and serve hot.

Serves 4

fish & seafood

Wherever you go around the Mediterranean coastline you are bound to be seduced by the sensual flavours of local seafood cooking in beachfront restaurants and bars. Fish is often served grilled or barbecued and bathed in a fragrant oil. Vegetable sauces thickened with nuts, like the Italian Salsa Rossa (see page 136), are the perfect accompaniment to chargrilled squid or barbecued sardines. When buying fish and seafood be sure to use a good fishmonger. Fish should smell of the sea and appear bright and firm. It is best eaten on the day it is bought.

hake with peppers

spain

4 tablespoons olive oil

4 small red peppers, cored, deseeded and thickly sliced

4 garlic cloves, peeled but left whole

2 thyme sprigs

pinch of hot paprika

75 ml (3 fl oz) dry sherry

4 potatoes

4–8 hake steaks, depending on the size of the fish (see right)

2 bay leaves

salt and pepper

To serve:

crusty bread

Aïoli (see page 134)

Hake is eaten all over the Mediterranean, with the Spanish and Portuguese being particularly fond of it. This recipe is based on a Spanish dish where the hake steaks are baked with potatoes and peppers, and would traditionally be served with aïoli. Allow 175 g (6 oz) hake steak per person, which may mean you will need eight small steaks.

1 Heat the oil in a flameproof casserole, add the peppers, garlic, thyme sprigs and paprika and fry over a gentle heat for 15–20 minutes, stirring frequently, until browned and softened. Add the sherry and boil rapidly until reduced by half.

2 Meanwhile, parboil the potatoes for 10–12 minutes, until nearly cooked. Refresh under cold water and cut into cubes.

3 Stir the potatoes into the pepper mixture with some salt and pepper. Season the hake steaks and arrange them on top, pressing them down into the peppers slightly. Add the bay leaves and 4 tablespoons of water, cover the casserole and simmer gently over a low heat for 15–20 minutes, depending on the thickness of the fish. Leave the fish to rest for a few minutes before serving with crusty bread and aïoli.

Serves 4

monkfish with raito

france

Raito is a Provençal tomato and red wine sauce, typically served with white fish. It is probable that this sauce, which is thickened with walnuts, was introduced to Provence by Phoenician traders. It is traditionally cooked at Christmas time.

1 First make the raito. Heat the oil in a saucepan and fry the onion, garlic and fennel seeds for 5 minutes, until the onion is softened, then add the tomatoes and fry for a further 5 minutes. Stir in the wine and boil rapidly for 5 minutes, until reduced slightly.

2 Add the water, tomato purée, sugar, thyme, rosemary, bay leaves and walnuts, bring to the boil and simmer gently for 1 hour. Remove the herbs and bay leaves and process the sauce in a food processor or blender until really smooth, then return to the pan and stir in the sun-dried tomatoes, capers, olives and salt and pepper to taste. Reheat gently and keep warm.

3 Season the monkfish fillets and wrap each one in a piece of ham, securing it in place with cocktail sticks. Heat the oil in a frying pan, add the fish and cook for 6–8 minutes, turning frequently, until evenly browned. Wrap the fish loosely in foil and leave to rest for 5 minutes.

4 Cut the fish into thick slices and serve with the raito.

Serves 4

4 x 250 g (8 oz) monkfish fillets

4 slices of Bayonne ham or Parma ham

2 tablespoons olive oil

salt and pepper

Raito:

4 tablespoons olive oil

1 onion, finely chopped

2 garlic cloves, crushed

2 teaspoons fennel seeds

500 g (1 lb) ripe vine tomatoes, chopped

300 ml (½ pint) red wine

150 ml (¼ pint) boiling water

1 tablespoon tomato purée

1 teaspoon sugar

2 thyme sprigs

2 rosemary sprigs

2 bay leaves

25 g (1 oz) shelled walnuts, toasted and ground

4 sun-dried tomatoes in oil, drained and chopped

2 tablespoon salted capers, rinsed

12 Niçoise olives

salt and pepper

seared tuna with muhammara

morocco

**4 tuna steaks, each about
75 g (6 oz)
a bunch of thyme
extra virgin olive oil
salt and pepper
rocket salad, to serve**

Muhammara:
**50 g (2 oz) walnuts
25 g (1 oz) fresh breadcrumbs
2 garlic cloves, crushed
1 tablespoon lemon juice
2 teaspoons pomegranate syrup
75 ml (3 fl oz) extra virgin olive oil
1–2 tablespoons boiling water
salt and pepper**

Muhammara is a North African walnut sauce similar to the Turkish tarator. The main difference is the addition of the sweet/sour pomegranate syrup to the North African version, which adds an exotic flavour that is unique.

1 Wash and dry the tuna and, using the thyme sprigs, rub all over with oil and season well with salt and pepper. Set aside.

2 To make the muhammara, place the walnuts, breadcrumbs, garlic, lemon juice, pomegranate syrup and salt and pepper in a food processor and pulse to form a fairly rough paste. Gradually blend in the oil until the sauce is amalgamated and fairly fine, adding a little boiling water to thin it slightly (it should have the texture of hummus). Taste and adjust the seasoning. Transfer the sauce to a bowl, cover the surface with clingfilm and leave to infuse for 30 minutes.

3 Heat a ridged griddle pan until really hot (this will take about 3 minutes), then add the tuna steaks and cook for 1 minute on each side, allowing a little longer if they are thick. Transfer the steaks to a plate, cover with foil and leave to rest for 3–4 minutes. Serve with the muhammara and a rocket salad.

Serves 4

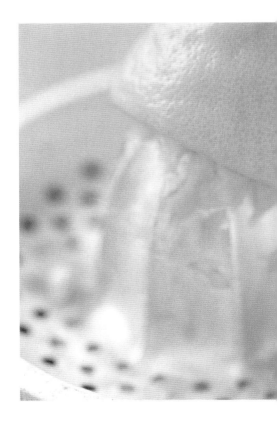

mullet with vine leaves

greece

6 tablespoons olive oil

2 tablespoons lemon juice

2 tablespoons chopped dill

2 spring onions, chopped

1 teaspoon mustard powder

8 vine leaves in brine, drained

4 red mullet, scaled and gutted

4 bay leaves

4 dill sprigs

salt and pepper

tomato and olive salad, to serve (optional)

To garnish:

lemon wedges

dill sprigs

Vine leaves, sometimes known as grape leaves, are widely used in Mediterranean dishes, especially in Greece and Turkey, where they have been used for centuries, long before the introduction of the lemon, to add acidity to dishes. Here they are wrapped around red mullet both to flavour the fish and keep it moist during cooking.

1 Put four pieces of string, about 30 cm (12 inches) long, into cold water to soak for 10 minutes.

2 In a bowl, combine the oil, lemon juice, chopped dill, spring onions, mustard powder and salt and pepper. Wash and dry the vine leaves and arrange them in pairs, overlapping them slightly.

3 Make several slashes on both sides of each fish and rub them all over with a little of the oil and lemon mixture. Stuff each of the belly cavities with a bay leaf and a dill sprig. Wrap each fish in a couple of vine leaves, brush with a little oil and fasten with the wet string to secure the leaves in place.

4 Grill, griddle or barbecue the fish for 4–5 minutes on each side, brushing them with a little more oil if necessary, until lightly charred. Leave the fish to rest for a few minutes, then discard the vine leaves and dress the mullet with the rest of the lemon oil. Garnish with lemon wedges and dill sprigs and serve with a tomato and olive salad, if liked.

Serves 4

scallop & monkfish skewers with fennel sauce

italy

Skewers of meat and fish (spiedini) *are popular all over Italy, especially during the summer months when the Italians cook on their barbecues all the time. It was at a fiesta one summer evening just south of Florence that I stopped to watch the festivities and nibble on moist, smoky skewers of seafood, making a very memorable night.*

4 dried fennel or oregano stalks, about 20 cm (8 inches) long

500 g (1 lb) monkfish fillets

8 large scallops

2 tablespoon olive oil

1 garlic clove, crushed

salt and pepper

bread, to serve

Fennel sauce:

3 tablespoons chopped fennel or dill fronds

pinch of dried chilli flakes

2 teaspoons lemon juice

6–8 tablespoons olive oil

1 fennel bulb

salt and pepper

1 Pull off the dried leaves still attached to the fennel or oregano stalks, leaving a clump at one end, and soak the stalks in cold water for at least 30 minutes.

2 Cut the monkfish into 12 large chunks about the same size as the scallops and place in a ceramic dish. Cut away the tough white muscle from each scallop and remove any intestine. Wash and pat dry and add to the monkfish.

3 Stir in the olive oil, garlic and some pepper until the seafood is thoroughly coated; cover and marinate for at least 30 minutes. Thread the pieces of seafood on to the herb stalks.

4 Meanwhile, make the fennel sauce. Mix together the fennel or dill fronds, chilli flakes, lemon juice, oil and season with salt and pepper to taste, cover and set aside to infuse. Just before serving, thinly slice the fennel bulb and toss with the sauce.

5 Season the seafood with salt and cook either on a barbecue or on a griddle for 5–6 minutes, turning the skewers halfway through and basting with the marinade, until charred and tender.

6 Serve the skewers hot, with the fennel sauce and some bread to mop up the juices.

Serves 4

provençal seafood stew with tomatoes & saffron

france

The flavours of saffron, orange and Pernod are so evocative of Provence I almost feel I'm there every time I cook this stew. It has become a favourite dinner party dish, as much of the work can be done ahead of time.

1 Peel and devein the prawns, reserving the heads and shells. Wash the prawns and dry well on kitchen paper.

2 Heat 2 tablespoons of the oil in a deep frying pan, add the prawn heads and shells and fry over a low heat for 10 minutes, then remove with a slotted spoon and discard. Add the remaining oil to the pan and sauté the onion, garlic, fennel seeds, thyme and orange rind for 10 minutes, until softened.

3 Add the tomatoes, stock, saffron, Pernod and some salt and pepper. Bring to the boil, cover the pan and simmer gently for 30 minutes, then remove the lid and cook for a further 15 minutes, until thickened slightly.

4 Cut each red mullet into 4–5 chunks and cut the tuna into similar sized pieces. Stir into the stew with the prawns, parsley and anchovies and simmer, covered, for a further 5–10 minutes, until all the seafood is cooked. Serve with pasta noodles.

Serves 6

12 large raw prawns

3 tablespoons extra virgin olive oil

1 onion, finely chopped

2 garlic cloves, crushed

1 teaspoon fennel seeds

2 teaspoons chopped thyme

grated rind of ½ orange

400 g (13 oz) can plum tomatoes, chopped

300 ml (½ pint) Fish Stock (see page 139)

pinch of saffron threads

4 tablespoons Pernod

3 red mullet, scaled and gutted

375 g (12 oz) tuna steak

2 tablespoons chopped parsley

2 salted anchovies, rinsed and chopped

salt and pepper

pasta noodles, to serve

stuffed squid with salsa rossa

italy

8 small squid, each about 12 cm (5 inches) long, cleaned

4 tablespoons olive oil

50 g (2 oz) smoked pancetta, diced

1 onion, chopped

2 garlic cloves, crushed

2 teaspoons chopped thyme

50 g (2 oz) sun-dried tomatoes in oil, drained and chopped

75 g (3 oz) fresh white breadcrumbs

2 tablespoons chopped basil

juice of ½ lemon

2 tablespoons water

salt and pepper

Salsa Rossa (see page 136)

green salad, to serve

Once cleaned, the bodies of small squid are perfect for stuffing, keeping the filling really moist as they cook. The pancetta can be omitted and replaced with 4 chopped anchovy fillets, if preferred. I also serve Romesco Sauce (page 134) or Pesto (page 138) with the squid, which work just as well as salsa rosso.

1 Discard the "beak" from the squid, remove the tentacles and chop them finely. Heat half of the oil in a frying pan and fry the pancetta for 5 minutes, until crisp and golden. Remove with a slotted spoon and reserve.

2 Add the onion, garlic, thyme, chopped tentacles and sun-dried tomatoes to the pan and fry gently for 5 minutes, until softened. Transfer to a food processor and pulse briefly until coarsely ground. Stir in the breadcrumbs, basil and lemon juice and season with salt and pepper to taste. Leave to cool completely.

3 Spoon the mixture into the cavity of the squid and secure the tops with cocktail sticks. Place the squid in a roasting tin, add the remaining oil and the water and roast in a preheated oven, 230°C (450°F), Gas Mark 8, for 20 minutes.

4 Meanwhile, prepare the salsa rossa. Serve the stuffed squid hot with the sauce and a crisp green salad.

Serves 4

gambas a la plancha

spain

In Spain, prawns and squid are often cooked very simply on a flat griddle. This method is known as a la plancha, and the wonderful smells that emanate from the kitchen when seafood is cooked in this way will forever be ingrained in my memory.

1 Remove the heads from the prawns but leave the shells intact. Place the bodies flat on a board with the shell uppermost and, using a sharp knife, carefully cut down along the whole length of the prawn, without cutting all the way through. Open the prawns out flat. (This is called butterflying.)

2 Discard the black vein from each prawn, then wash the prawns and pat dry. Place the prawns in a large bowl, add the garlic, chilli and olive oil with a little salt and pepper. Cover and marinate for at least 1 hour.

3 Heat a griddle for 3 minutes, until really hot. Add the prawns, shell side down, and fry for 3–4 minutes, in batches, until the flesh is cooked through. Turn them over and cook the second side for a few seconds. Transfer the cooked prawns to a large, warmed platter, drizzle over plenty of oil and serve with lemon wedges for squeezing and some crusty bread to mop up the juices.

Serves 4

1 kg (2 lb) large raw prawns

4 garlic cloves, sliced

1 red chilli, deseeded and chopped

4 tablespoons extra virgin olive oil, plus extra to serve

salt and pepper

lemon wedges, to garnish

crusty bread, to serve

barbecued sardines

spain

Sardines are popular throughout the Mediterranean and are particularly favoured by the Spanish (almost as much as the Portuguese). The most important factor when choosing sardines is their freshness; they must not be tired or limp but bright, shiny and firm. Ask your fishmonger to scale but not gut the fish as this can tear the skin.

1 First skin the peppers. Put the whole peppers under a preheated hot grill and cook until charred all over, then transfer them to a plastic bag and leave to cool. Peel and discard the skin and seeds, and cut the flesh into thin strips, mixing them with some oil, vinegar and sea salt and pepper.

2 Meanwhile, wash and dry the sardines, place them on a large platter and sprinkle liberally with sea salt. Cover and set aside for 1 hour. Wash and dry again, brush with a little oil and barbecue, griddle or grill for 2–3 minutes on each side, until cooked through. Serve the sardines hot with the peppers and a tomato salad.

Serves 4

2 red peppers

extra virgin olive oil

white wine vinegar

16 fresh sardines, scaled but not gutted (see left)

sea salt and pepper

tomato salad, to serve

roast lobsters with garlic sauce

greece

4 whole lobsters, each about
500 g (1 lb), cut in half

8 large rosemary sprigs, about
15 cm (6 inches) long

salt and pepper

Garlic sauce:

200 ml (7 fl oz) extra virgin olive oil

4 red chillies, deseeded and finely
chopped

4 garlic cloves, crushed

2 tablespoons snipped rosemary

juice of 1 lemon

salt and pepper

It was on my honeymoon on the Greek island of Lesvos that I ate the most sublime lobster, grilled and served with garlic sauce. I have experimented with grilling, barbecuing and roasting lobsters and I think the easiest and most successful way of cooking them is to roast them in a really hot oven. Unfortunately, for the best results, the lobster must be cut in half while alive, so thank goodness for fishmongers.

1 First prepare the garlic sauce. Mix together all the ingredients in a bowl and season with salt and pepper to taste.

2 Using a mallet or rolling pin, crack the claws of each lobster to aid the cooking process.

3 Using half of the sprigs, make a bed of rosemary in a shallow roasting dish and place the lobsters, shell side down, on top. Spoon over a little of the sauce, season with salt and pepper and cover with the remaining rosemary. Roast in a preheated oven, 240°C (475°F), Gas Mark 9, for 15 minutes.

4 Allow the lobster to rest for a few minutes, then serve with the remaining garlic sauce.

Serves 4

poultry & game

Many Mediterranean households keep chickens and, although the birds may appear a little scrawny, their flesh is generally tender and moist. Chicken is usually roasted or stewed; it is an everyday food and is rarely served on special occasions. When possible, buy free-range organic fowl from a reliable butcher. Birds like duck are bred for the table, but the majority of game is hunted; rabbit, partridge and wild boar being the favourites.

chicken, lemon & olive stew

morocco

2.25 kg (4½ lb) free-range chicken

about 4 tablespoons olive oil

12 baby onions, peeled but left whole

2 garlic cloves, crushed

1 teaspoon each ground cumin, ginger and turmeric

½ teaspoon ground cinnamon

450 ml (¾ pint) Chicken Stock (see page 139)

125 g (4 oz) Kalamata olives

1 preserved lemon, chopped

2 tablespoons chopped coriander

salt and pepper

cooked couscous, rice or pasta, to serve

This is a Moroccan dish using preserved lemons, a bitter pickle which is added to many of their meat dishes. There is a recipe for Preserved Lemons on page 140. Alternatively, they can be bought from North African and Middle Eastern stores and some supermarkets.

1 Joint the chicken into eight pieces (or ask your butcher to do this for you). Heat the oil in a flameproof casserole and brown the chicken on all sides. Remove the pieces with a slotted spoon and set aside.

2 Add the onions, garlic and spices and sauté over a low heat for 10 minutes, until just golden. Return the chicken to the pan, stir in the stock and bring to the boil. Cover and simmer gently for 30 minutes.

3 Add the olives, chopped lemon and coriander and cook for a further 15–20 minutes, until the chicken is really tender. Taste and adjust the seasoning, if necessary and serve with couscous, rice or pasta.

Serves 4

boiled chicken with aïoli

france

1.5 kg (3 lb) free-range chicken

1 onion, studded with 3 cloves

250 g (8 oz) piece of smoked pancetta

4 Toulouse or good quality pork sausages

4 carrots, trimmed

4 leeks, trimmed

bouquet garni

4 waxy potatoes

1 small green cabbage, cut into wedges

2 tablespoons chopped parsley

salt and pepper

To serve:

1 quantity Aïoli (see page 134)

crusty bread

Poule au pot is the French method of cooking a whole chicken in water with a mixture of vegetables and other meats, typically bacon and sausages. By the time the chicken is tender, the vegetables and meats are cooked and the stock is full of all the different flavours. The meat and vegetables are served on a plate with the sauce passed around separately.

1 Wash and dry the chicken and stuff the cavity with the studded onion. Place in a large flameproof casserole, cover with cold water and bring to the boil, removing the scum as it rises to the surface.

2 Add the pancetta, sausages, carrots, leeks and bouquet garni and return to the boil. Simmer gently, partially covered, for 20 minutes, then add the potatoes and cabbage and continue to simmer for a further 40 minutes, until all the vegetables and meats are tender.

3 When the meats are tender, carefully remove them from the casserole and place on a warmed platter with the vegetables. Cover with foil and transfer to a low oven to keep warm. Strain the poaching stock into a clean pan and boil rapidly until reduced by half. Season with salt and pepper and stir in the parsley.

4 Carve the meats and arrange in individual soup plates with the vegetables. Pour over some of the stock and serve with a good spoonful of aïoli and some crusty bread.

Serves 4

pigeon with fresh peas

italy

An Italian casserole, from Umbria, of whole pigeons cooked with peas. Use frozen petit pois if young fresh peas are unavailable.

1 Wash and dry the pigeons inside and out. Wrap 2 rashers of pancetta around each pigeon and tie in place with string.

2 Heat the oil in a flameproof casserole and brown the pigeons on all sides, then remove them with a slotted spoon. Add the onions and sauté for 5 minutes, until golden.

3 Return the pigeons to the pan, breast side down, add the wine and boil rapidly until reduced by half. Pour in the stock, add the thyme, cover and bake in a preheated oven, 180°C (350°F), Gas Mark 4, for 45–60 minutes, until the pigeons are tender.

4 Add the peas and transfer the casserole to the hob. Simmer, uncovered, for about 10–15 minutes until the peas are tender. Remove the pigeons to a warmed plate and wrap in foil to rest for 5 minutes. Lower the heat and whisk in the butter a little at a time, season with salt and pepper to taste and serve the peas and sauce with the pigeons.

Serves 4

4 oven-ready pigeons

8 rashers smoked pancetta

4 tablespoons olive oil

250 g (8 oz) tiny baby onions, peeled but left whole

150 ml (¼ pint) dry white wine

300 ml (½ pint) Chicken Stock (see page 139)

2 teaspoons chopped thyme

250 g (8 oz) shelled peas

50 g (2 oz) butter, diced

salt and pepper

lemon chicken with yogurt sauce

greece

Some of the best meals you can eat in Greece are the grilled or barbecued meats, my particular favourite being grilled chicken. It is always tender, moist and very tasty.

1 Wash and dry the chicken quarters and rub all over, quite hard, with the cut lemons. Place the chicken in a large ceramic dish, add the oregano, thyme, olive oil, garlic and the rubbed lemon halves and stir well. Cover and marinate for at least 2 hours.

2 Meanwhile, make the yogurt sauce. Pour the yogurt into a bowl and beat. Pound together the garlic and salt either using a pestle and mortar or on a chopping board with the side of a knife blade. Stir into the yogurt with the dill. Set aside until required.

3 Remove the chicken pieces and lemon halves from the dish, reserving the marinade. Cook, either over hot coals or under a preheated hot grill, at least 12 cm (5 inches) below the heat source, for 30 minutes, basting occasionally with the reserved marinade and turning halfway through, until charred and cooked through. Serve with the yogurt sauce and chips.

Serves 4

4 chicken quarters

2 lemons, halved

1 tablespoon dried oregano

2 thyme sprigs

4 tablespoons extra virgin olive oil

4 garlic cloves, roughly chopped

chips, to serve

Yogurt sauce:

250 ml (8 fl oz) Greek yogurt

1–2 garlic cloves

½ teaspoon sea salt

1 tablespoon chopped dill

pot-roast partridge with lentils

france

250 g (8 oz) green lentils

4 oven-ready partridges

50 g (2 oz) butter

1 onion, finely chopped

2 garlic cloves

1 tablespoon chopped thyme

1 carrot, diced

1 leek, diced

1 celery stick, diced

4 bay leaves

6 juniper berries

300 ml (½ pint) red wine

600 ml (1 pint) Chicken Stock (see page 139)

To garnish:

celery leaves

chopped parsley

thyme sprigs

The hills of Provence provide a wide variety of game birds, but this dish of partridge braised with lentils probably originated slightly further west towards Gascony. It is enjoyed during the winter months when heartier dishes are cooked.

1 Soak the lentils in cold water for 1 hour, then drain in a colander and shake dry.

2 Remove the giblets, if any, from the partridges and discard. Melt half of the butter in a flameproof casserole and brown the partridges all over. Remove with a slotted spoon and set aside.

3 Add the remaining butter to the casserole and gently fry the onion, garlic, thyme and vegetables for 10 minutes until softened. Add the bay leaves and juniper berries, pour in the wine and boil rapidly until reduced by half.

4 Return the birds and giblets to the casserole with the stock and bring to the boil. Cover the casserole, transfer to a preheated oven, 190°C (375°F), Gas Mark 5, and pot-roast for 45 minutes.

5 Carefully remove the lid and tip in the lentils, making sure they fall around the birds. Cover the casserole and return to the oven for 1 hour, until the partridges and lentils are tender. Remove the birds, cover with foil and leave to rest for 10 minutes before carving. Serve garnished with the celery leaves, parsley and thyme.

Serves 4

duck with pears

spain

2.25 kg (4½ lb) duck, quartered

1 Spanish onion, chopped

2 garlic cloves, crushed

200 ml (7 fl oz) Chicken Stock
(see page 139)

2 tablespoons Spanish brandy

2 tablespoons raisins

2 tablespoons unblanched almonds

6 juniper berries, bruised

4 pears, peeled and halved

1 tablespoon sherry vinegar

salt and pepper

boiled rice or potatoes, to serve

Duck with pears is a classic Spanish dish from Catalonia. I find that cooking the bird over two days results in a tastier and more tender dish, and the fat is easier to remove when it is cold.

1 Prick the duck pieces all over with a skewer and place them in a roasting tin, skin side up. Roast in a preheated oven, 200°C (400°F), Gas Mark 6, for 45 minutes, until crisp. Pour off as much of the duck fat as you can, being careful to leave the juices behind. Reserve 2 tablespoons of the fat.

2 Heat the reserved duck fat in a flameproof casserole, add the onion and garlic and fry gently for 10 minutes until lightly golden. Stir in the stock, brandy, raisins, almonds and juniper berries and bring to the boil. Add the duck and the pan juices, cover and simmer for 30 minutes. Leave to cool then refrigerate overnight.

3 The next day, remove the duck from the refrigerator and scrape off all the fat that has set on the surface of the stew. Place the casserole on the heat and bring slowly to the boil. Add the pear halves and vinegar, season with salt and pepper to taste, cover and simmer gently for about 20 minutes, until the pears are cooked and the duck is tender. Serve with boiled rice or potatoes.

Serves 4

poussins baked with pistachios

tunisia

1 onion, sliced

4 garlic cloves, roughly chopped

4 ripe tomatoes, chopped

125 g (4 oz) shelled pistachio nuts

50 g (2 oz) sultanas

2 x 500 g (1 lb) poussins

1 tablespoon olive oil

pinch of saffron threads

½ teaspoon each ground cumin, ginger, turmeric and cinnamon

300 ml (½ pint) Chicken Stock
(see page 139)

salt and pepper

The combination of spices, nuts and fruit in this dish indicates that it probably originated in North Africa, although I ate a similar dish in a Spanish restaurant in New York.

1 Place the onion, garlic, tomatoes, pistachio nuts and sultanas in a deep casserole with a little salt and pepper.

2 Wash and dry the poussins thoroughly and sit them on top of the vegetables and drizzle over the oil. Stir the saffron and spices into the hot stock and pour it around the poussins. Cover the casserole and bake in a preheated oven, 200°C (400°F), Gas Mark 6, for 40 minutes.

3 Remove the lid of the casserole and baste the poussins with the pan juices. Bake for a further 30 minutes, until they are browned and the leg juices run clear when pierced with a skewer. Serve hot.

Serves 4

hunter-style rabbit stew

italy

A simple peasant dish, said to be a favourite of Tuscan hunters, who would no doubt have skinned and barbecued their prize over a camp fire with little more than a few wild herbs to rub over the meat as it cooked. This recipe is a little more sophisticated than that, but still remains straightforward.

1 Wash and dry the rabbit pieces and liver and place in a ceramic dish with the garlic, rosemary, sage, red wine and a good seasoning of salt and pepper. Cover and leave to marinate overnight.

2 Remove the rabbit pieces and the liver from the marinade and dry well on kitchen paper. Strain the marinade into a saucepan, bring to the boil and simmer until reduced by half, then strain through a fine sieve.

3 Heat the oil in a flameproof casserole, add the rabbit and liver and brown on all sides. Add the reduced marinade, tomatoes and tomato purée. Bring to the boil and simmer gently, covered, for 1 hour, adding the olives for the final 15 minutes. Remove the rabbit to a warmed plate, wrap loosely in foil and keep warm.

4 Mash the liver into the sauce, return to the boil and boil for 10 minutes until the sauce is thick and glossy. Pour the sauce over the rabbit and serve with soft polenta or pappardelle noodles.

Serves 4

1 rabbit, cut into 8 joints, reserving the liver

2 garlic cloves, crushed

1 tablespoon each chopped rosemary and sage

1 bottle dry red wine

2 tablespoons olive oil

500 g (1 lb) ripe tomatoes, skinned, deseeded and chopped

2 tablespoons tomato purée

12 Tuscan black olives

salt and pepper

soft polenta or pappardelle noodles, to serve

meat dishes

Meat tends to be treated as a luxury food, although lamb and pork are plentiful. Beef is rare but veal is popular in Italy, Spain and Greece. Pork is prohibited by the Muslim and Jewish religions but elsewhere, particularly in Spain, Greece and Italy, it is cooked widely. Stews, roasts and grills are common and meat sauces are often served with the staple food of the region, such as pasta and couscous. Try to use good quality, free-range meat, whenever possible.

daube of beef

france

This slow cooked beef stew flavoured with Provençal olives makes a rich winter dish.

1 First make the marinade. Heat the oil in a saucepan and fry the onion, carrots, celery and thyme for 10 minutes. Pour in the wine, bring to the boil and simmer gently for 20 minutes. Leave to cool completely, then add the beef and marinate overnight.

2 The next day, transfer the beef to a flameproof casserole, reserving the marinade, and top with the baby onions, garlic, carrots, celery, orange peel, herbs, tomatoes, tomato purée, stock and some salt and pepper.

3 Strain the reserved marinade into the casserole, bring to the boil and cover with a tight-fitting lid. Transfer the casserole to a preheated oven, 150°C (300°F), Gas Mark 2, and cook for 2 hours.

4 Remove the casserole from the oven and stir in the anchovies and olives, season with salt and pepper to taste and return to the oven for 1 hour, until the beef is really tender. Leave the casserole to cool completely, then refrigerate overnight. Skim the surface of any fat from the surface and reheat well before serving.

Serves 4–6

1 kg (2 lb) braising steak, cubed

250 g (8 oz) baby onions, peeled and left whole

2 garlic cloves, crushed

2 carrots, thickly sliced

2 celery sticks, thickly sliced

4 strips of orange peel

2 bay leaves

2 thyme sprigs

2 rosemary sprigs

400 g (13 oz) can chopped tomatoes

2 tablespoons tomato purée

300 ml (½ pint) beef stock

4 salted anchovy fillets, rinsed and chopped

50 g (2 oz) Niçoise olives

salt and pepper

Marinade:

2 tablespoons olive oil

1 onion, chopped

2 carrots, chopped

2 celery sticks, chopped

1 tablespoon chopped thyme

450 ml (¾ pint) red wine

lamb tagine with fig couscous

morocco

In Moroccan cooking, an earthenware dish with a conical lid, called a tagine, is used to cook all manner of meat, poultry and fish stews. These fragrant stews have become one of the country's national treasures. Traditionally, they are served with couscous, a pasta-like grain that is steamed over the stew as it cooks, imparting the delicious flavours into the couscous.

1 kg (2 lb) lamb neck fillet, cubed

2 onions, chopped

4 garlic cloves, crushed

1 teaspoon each paprika and ground ginger

½ teaspoon each cayenne pepper and ground turmeric

1 cinnamon stick, roughly crumbled

¼ teaspoon chilli flakes

400 g (13 oz) can chickpeas, drained

2 potatoes, diced

2 carrots, sliced

125 g (4 oz) dried figs, sliced

2 courgettes, sliced

2 tablespoons chopped coriander

salt and pepper

To serve:

250 g (8 oz) couscous

Harissa (see page 32)

1 Put the lamb, onions, garlic, spices and chilli flakes into the bottom of a double boiler with a little salt and pepper and then add enough water to cover completely. Bring to the boil, cover and simmer gently for 1½ hours.

2 Stir in the chickpeas, potatoes, carrots, figs, courgettes and coriander, cover and cook for a further 20–30 minutes, until all the vegetables and meat are tender.

3 Meanwhile, soak the couscous in warm water for 10 minutes, then drain.

4 Ten minutes before the stew is ready, place the couscous in the top of the double boiler and steam until the grains are puffed up and softened. As soon as the stew is cooked, serve with the couscous and some harissa.

Serves 4

lamb steaks baked in foil

turkey

This dish is based on a Turkish recipe, supplied to me by a friend from Istanbul, but I have adapted it slightly. The meat and vegetables are first stewed and then wrapped in foil in individual portions and baked until the meat is meltingly tender. The kasar cheese used is a ewe's milk cheese and can be found in Turkish food stores. If you cannot find it, use pecorino sardo instead.

1 Season the steaks well with salt and pepper. Melt the butter in a flameproof casserole and brown the steaks on both sides. Remove with a slotted spoon.

2 Add the onion, potatoes and carrots to the pan and fry gently for 10 minutes, until lightly golden. Add the lamb with the tomatoes, bay leaves, dill, spices, water and salt and pepper. Bring to the boil, cover and simmer gently for 1 hour.

3 Carefully arrange a steak and a quarter of the vegetables in the middle of each of 4 large sheets of foil, adding some of the pan juices. Wrap up the parcels and cook in a preheated oven, 190°C (375°F), Gas Mark 5, for a further 30 minutes.

4 Open the parcels, place a slice of cheese in each, allowing it to melt before serving.

Serves 4

4 lamb leg steaks, each about 300 g (10 oz)

50 g (2 oz) butter

1 onion, sliced

2 large potatoes, thickly sliced

2 large carrots, chopped

2 tomatoes, roughly chopped

4 bay leaves

1 tablespoon chopped dill

½ teaspoon ground allspice

pinch of ground cinnamon

150 ml (¼ pint) water

50 g (2 oz) kasar cheese, sliced into 4 pieces

salt and pepper

pan-fried veal with caper sauce

italy

Thin escalopes of veal are seared in butter and then briefly braised with capers, wine and balsamic vinegar for a quick supper dish. I have served this dish for 2 people as frying pans are really only wide enough to take two escalopes at a time.

1 Place the escalopes between two sheets of clingfilm and using a mallet or rolling pin, beat until they are about 3 mm (⅛ inch) thick. Season with salt and pepper on both sides.

2 Melt half of the butter in a large frying pan. When the foam dies down, add the veal and fry for 30 seconds on each side, until lightly golden. Add the capers, wine, vinegar and parsley and simmer for 1 minute.

3 Transfer the veal to warmed plates. Lower the heat and gradually whisk in the remaining butter. Season with salt and pepper to taste and pour the pan juices over the veal. Serve immediately.

Serves 2

2 veal escalopes, each about 150 g (5 oz)

50 g (2 oz) unsalted butter, diced

2 tablespoons salted capers, washed and dried

50 ml (2 fl oz) dry white wine

1 tablespoon balsamic vinegar

2 tablespoons chopped parsley

salt and pepper

butterflied leg of lamb with roasted garlic

italy

2 kg (4 lb) leg of lamb, boned and butterflied (see right)

2 garlic cloves, crushed

4 rosemary sprigs

4 thyme sprigs

grated rind and juice of 1 lemon

5 tablespoons olive oil

6 whole heads of garlic

salt and pepper

rosemary sprigs, to garnish

Slow–roasted Tomatoes (see page 45), to serve

Ask your butcher to bone and butterfly the lamb for you. This is an excellent method of cooking a leg of lamb, particularly on the barbecue, as the meat cooks far quicker without the bone. The flavours are Italian and this dish is great served with Slow–roasted Tomatoes (see page 45). The tomatoes can be cooked ahead of time and reheated with the garlic for the final 10 minutes of cooking time.

1 Place the lamb in a deep bowl, add the crushed garlic, herb sprigs, some salt and pepper and the lemon rind and rub into the flesh. Add the lemon juice and 4 tablespoons of the oil, cover and leave in the refrigerator to marinate overnight.

2 Return the lamb to room temperature.

3 Take the whole garlic heads and cut off the tops, exposing the cloves. Drizzle each one with a little of the remaining oil and wrap the heads in individual foil parcels. Bake in a preheated oven, 200°C (400°F), Gas Mark 6, for 45–50 minutes, until tender. Keep warm.

4 Remove the lamb from the marinade and dry well on kitchen paper. Cook over hot coals, under a preheated hot grill or on a ridged griddle pan for 12–15 minutes on each side, depending on the thickness of the meat and how pink you like it. Cover with foil and leave to rest for 10 minutes.

5 Serve the lamb in slices, garnished with rosemary sprigs and accompanied by the heads of garlic and the slow–roasted tomatoes.

Serves 6

catalan beef stew with chocolate

spain

25 g (1 oz) butter

5 tablespoons olive oil

1 kg (2 lb) stewing beef, cubed

2 onions, chopped

4 garlic cloves, chopped

1 tablespoon plain flour

150 ml (¼ pint) dry sherry

4 parsley sprigs

4 bay leaves

1 teaspoon each dried oregano and thyme

2 cinnamon sticks, crumbled

250 g (8 oz) button mushrooms

15 g (½ oz) bitter chocolate, chopped

250 g (8 oz) waxy potatoes, cubed

2 good quality pork sausages

salt and pepper

The use of chocolate in a savoury dish usually implies that the recipe originates from the Catalan region of Spain. Chocolate adds both a richness and slight tartness to this stew, although traditionally the type of chocolate used would contain cinnamon and rice flour as well as sugar and cocoa. It would be more authentic to use a slightly sweeter plain chocolate, but I prefer this stew cooked with really bitter chocolate.

1 Heat the butter and 2 tablespoons of the oil in a flameproof casserole, add the beef in batches and brown well on all sides. Stir in the onions and garlic and fry gently for a further 10 minutes, until they have softened, adding a little extra butter if necessary.

2 Sprinkle over the flour, stirring with a wooden spoon, and then gradually stir in the sherry. Bring to the boil and then add the herbs, cinnamon, a little salt and pepper and enough water to just cover the beef. Simmer gently, covered, for 2 hours.

3 Heat 2 tablespoons of the remaining oil in a frying pan and fry the mushrooms for 3–4 minutes, until browned, then stir them into the stew with the chocolate and potatoes. Cook for a further 20–30 minutes, until the beef and potatoes are tender. Season with salt and pepper to taste.

4 Just before serving, slice the sausages and fry briefly in the remaining oil until golden. Serve with the stew.

Serves 4

roast loin of pork

france

The addition of anchovies to the sauce for this pork roast is typical of Provençal cooking and can be found in many Provençal dishes. Serve the pork with roast potatoes and a selection of seasonal vegetables.

1 Wash and dry the pork and rub all over with the oil, then the coriander and salt and pepper, to coat with a thin layer of spice. Pierce the skin all over and stud with rosemary leaves and garlic slices.

2 Transfer the pork to a roasting tin with the wine and bay leaves and roast in a preheated oven, 200°C (400°F), Gas Mark 6, for 1½–2 hours, until the juices run clear when the pork is pierced with a knife. Remove the meat, set it on a warmed platter, wrap loosely in foil and leave to rest for 10 minutes.

3 Meanwhile, strain the juices into a pan and add the stock, lemon juice and anchovies. Bring to the boil and boil until reduced by half and thickened slightly. Taste and adjust the seasoning, if necessary and serve the sauce with the carved pork.

Serves 6

1.5 kg (3 lb) rolled loin of pork

2 tablespoons olive oil

2 tablespoons coriander seeds, lightly crushed

6–8 rosemary sprigs

4 garlic cloves, thickly sliced

125 ml (4 fl oz) dry white wine

2 bay leaves

300 ml (½ pint) Chicken Stock (see page 139)

juice of ½ lemon

2 canned anchovy fillets, drained and chopped

salt and pepper

1 tablespoon coriander seeds

4–6 tablespoons olive oil

1 kg (2 lb) boneless pork shoulder, cubed

2 onions, finely chopped

2 garlic cloves, crushed

300 ml (½ pint) red wine

2 tablespoons clear honey

150 ml (¼ pint) water

2 tablespoons tomato purée

2 teaspoons coarsely ground black peppercorns

2 cinnamon sticks, crumbled

¼ teaspoon whole cloves

750 g (1½ lb) quinces, peeled, cored and cut into chunks

salt

mashed potato, to serve (optional)

pork with quinces

greece/cyprus

This recipe is a bit of a hybrid, with influences from Greece and Cyprus. In Greece, quinces are paired with most types of meat, including lamb and veal. I prefer them with pork. The use of coriander seeds is typical of the Cypriot style of cooking known as afelia.

1 Dry-fry the coriander seeds in a heavy-based frying pan until toasted. Leave to cool, then grind coarsely.

2 Heat half of the oil in a frying pan and fry the pork, in batches, until browned. Transfer to a flameproof casserole with a slotted spoon. Add the onions and garlic to the frying pan, with a little more oil if necessary, and fry gently for 10 minutes. Add to the casserole with the wine, honey, water, tomato purée, coriander seeds, peppercorns, cinnamon, cloves and some salt.

3 Bring the stew to the boil, then cover the casserole and bake in a preheated oven, 180°C (350°F), Gas Mark 4, for 1½ hours.

4 Heat the remaining oil in a clean frying pan and fry the quinces for 5 minutes, until golden all over. Add to the pork, stirring well, and cook for a further 30–45 minutes, until both the meat and quinces are tender. Taste and adjust the seasoning, if necessary. Serve with mashed potato, if liked.

Serves 4

italian sausages with wet polenta & salsa rossa

italy

If you have eaten Italian sausages, then you will know how fantastic they can be. This recipe came to me through a friend of a friend from Sienna and it is delicious. If you don't fancy stuffing sausage skins yourself, you could try asking a local butcher who make their own sausages, to do this for you.

1 Drain the sausage skins and pat dry on kitchen paper.

2 Roast the fennel seeds in a small frying pan for 1–2 minutes, until browned and starting to pop. Leave to cool, then grind coarsely.

3 Put the meat into a food processor in small batches and, using the pulse button, process until roughly minced but not ground. Carefully pick out any large pieces of fat or gristle and discard. Tip the pork into a large bowl and work in the remaining ingredients.

4 Transfer the sausage filling to an icing bag fitted with a large plain nozzle and, holding the skin in place with one hand, squeeze the mixture into the sausage skins, twisting them into normal sausage lengths as you go, to make 12–16 small sausages. Separate into individual links.

5 Grill or fry the sausages for 15–20 minutes, until cooked. Keep them warm in a low oven while cooking the polenta.

6 To cook the polenta, bring the water to a rolling boil in a large saucepan. Add the salt and then carefully whisk in the polenta in a steady stream. Continue to beat with a wooden spoon over a low heat for 5 minutes until it is the texture of porridge. Beat in the sage, butter and Parmesan, season with salt and pepper to taste and spoon on to warmed plates. Top with the sausages and serve with a spoonful of salsa rossa.

Serves 4

25 g (1 oz) sausage skins, soaked in water for 2 hours

1½ tablespoons fennel seeds

375 g (12 oz) boneless pork shoulder, diced

375 g (12 oz) pork belly, diced

150 g (5 oz) neck lamb fillet, diced

100 g (3½ oz) pancetta, diced

2 garlic cloves, crushed

4 tablespoons chopped sage

1½ tablespoons lightly crushed black peppercorns

salt

Salsa Rossa (see page 136), to serve

Polenta:

1.5 litres (2½ pints) water

2 teaspoons salt

150 g (5 oz) instant polenta

1 tablespoon chopped sage

50 g (2 oz) butter

25 g (1 oz) Parmesan cheese, freshly grated

pepper

pork fillet with marsala

italy

Traditionally this dish would have been made with veal escalopes or pork medallions, but I like to pan-roast pork tenderloin and serve it in thick slices coated with the Marsala sauce just before serving. The crisp sage leaves are a fun addition, but can be omitted if you prefer.

1 Season the pork well with salt and pepper. Heat the oil in a large, ovenproof frying pan, add the meat and fry for about 5 minutes, until well browned on all sides. Transfer to a preheated oven, 190°C (375°F), Gas Mark 5, and roast for about 20 minutes, until the pork is cooked through. To test, push a skewer into the centre of the meat; the juices should run clear.

2 Remove the pork from the pan and and wrap it in foil to rest while making the sauce. Add 25 g (1 oz) of the butter to the pan and gently fry the shallots, garlic and sage for 5 minutes, until softened.

3 Deglaze the pan with the Marsala by boiling rapidly for 1–2 minutes, until slightly reduced, then add the stock and simmer for 5 minutes. Reduce the heat and gradually whisk in the remaining butter, a little at a time, until the sauce is thickened and glossy.

4 Heat a little oil in a separate pan and deep-fry the sage leaves, if using, for about 30 seconds, until crisp, then drain on kitchen paper.

5 Cut the pork into slices, pour over the sauce and garnish with sage leaves, if using. Serve with buttered spinach or greens with lemon oil (see page 52).

Serves 4

2 x 375 g (12 oz) pork tenderloins, trimmed

2 tablespoons olive oil

75 g (3 oz) butter, diced

2 shallots, finely chopped

1 small garlic clove, crushed

2 teaspoons chopped sage

125 ml (4 fl oz) Marsala

150 ml (¼ pint) Chicken Stock (see page 139)

salt and pepper

sage leaves, deep-fried in a little olive oil, to garnish (optional)

buttered spinach or Greens with Lemon Oil (see page 52), to serve

pasta, grains, rice & pulses

Staples such as pasta, rice, bulgar wheat and couscous provide the backbone of the Mediterranean diet and are eaten daily. They are served as an accompaniment to a main dish, or with a sauce, as well as forming the basis of other dishes such as Lemon, Leek & Bay Leaf Risotto (see page 102) or Chickpea & Rice Pilaf (see page 105). Pulses add bulk and are often combined with meat to 'stretch' it. Pasta, bulgar wheat and rice are used to thicken soups.

charred asparagus with lemon, basil & spaghetti

italy

This is a Californian recipe inspired by the flavours of Italy and it has become my absolute favourite. It is just such a pity that asparagus has such a short season, but in this recipe I often substitute broccoli instead.

500 g (1 lb) thin asparagus spears, trimmed

3–4 tablespoons extra virgin olive oil

juice of 1 lemon

375 g (12 oz) dried spaghetti

2 garlic cloves, roughly chopped

¼–½ teaspoon dried chilli flakes

25 g (1 oz) basil leaves

25 g (1 oz) freshly grated Parmesan cheese, plus extra to serve

salt and pepper

1 Brush the asparagus spears with a little oil and griddle or grill them until charred and tender. Toss with a little more oil, half of the lemon juice and salt and pepper and set aside.

2 Put a large pan of lightly salted boiling water on to boil, plunge in the pasta, return to the boil and cook according to the packet instructions until al dente.

3 Just before the pasta is cooked, heat the remaining oil in a large frying pan or wok and sauté the garlic with a little salt for 3–4 minutes, until softened but not browned. Add the chilli flakes and asparagus and heat through.

4 Drain the pasta, reserving 4 tablespoons of the cooking liquid, and add both to the pan with the basil, the remaining lemon juice, pepper and Parmesan. Serve immediately, with extra Parmesan, if liked.

Serves 4

fusilli with broad beans, parma ham & mint

italy

500 g (1 lb) shelled broad beans

375 g (12 oz) dried fusilli or other pasta shapes

4 tablespoons extra virgin olive oil

2 garlic cloves, finely chopped

150 ml (¼ pint) dry white wine

200 ml (7 fl oz) single cream

2 tablespoons chopped mint

4 slices of Parma ham, cut into thin strips

25 g (1 oz) pecorino sardo or Parmesan cheese, freshly grated

salt and pepper

freshly grated pecorino or Parmesan cheese, to serve

You can use any variety of dried pasta for this dish; I just happen to prefer fusilli in this particular recipe. Skinning the shelled beans is slightly laborious, but well worth the effort.

1 Plunge the beans into a large saucepan of lightly salted boiling water and boil for 1 minute; drain and immediately refresh under cold water. Carefully peel away and discard the rather tough outer skins of the beans.

2 Put a large pan of lightly salted water on to boil. Plunge the pasta into the boiling water, return to the boil and cook according to packet instructions until al dente.

3 Meanwhile, heat the oil in a deep frying pan and gently fry the garlic until softened, but not browned. Add the wine, boil rapidly until it is reduced to about 2 tablespoons, then stir in the cream, mint and pepper and heat through.

4 Drain the pasta and add to the sauce with the Parma ham and pecorino or Parmesan. Stir over the heat for about 30 seconds and serve with extra cheese.

Serves 4

pasta with sardines & sultanas

sicily

4 tablespoons sultanas

375 g (12 oz) dried penne

4 tablespoons extra virgin olive oil

4 garlic cloves, crushed

2 x 115 g (3¾ oz) cans sardines in olive oil, drained and chopped

2 tablespoons lemon juice

2 tablespoons toasted pine nuts

2 tablespoons salted capers, rinsed

4 tablespoons chopped parsley

salt and pepper

extra virgin olive oil, to serve

1 Soak the sultanas in a little hot water for 30 minutes, then drain and pat dry.

2 Put a large saucepan of lightly salted water on to boil. Plunge in the pasta, return to the boil and cook according to packet instructions until al dente.

3 Meanwhile, heat the oil in a frying pan, add the garlic and sauté gently until softened, but not browned. Add the sardines and lemon juice and cook, mashing the fish, for 1 minute. Stir in the nuts, capers, sultanas, parsley and salt and pepper to taste.

4 Drain the pasta, reserving 4 tablespoons of the cooking water, and add them both to the sauce, stirring over the heat for several seconds to coat the pasta. Taste and adjust the seasoning, if necessary and serve immediately drizzled with extra virgin olive oil.

Serves 4

pasta triangles with pumpkin & sage

italy

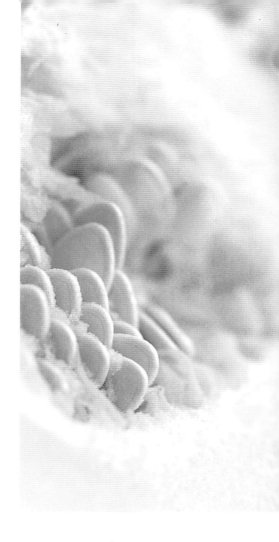

Homemade fresh pasta is so superior to any which is commercially available that making your own is a must. With the aid of a pasta machine, it is simple and incredibly satisfying. After a little practice, you will be able to get your pasta sheets almost paper thin, for a delicate, light result.

1 Place the pumpkin in a small roasting tin with the garlic, sage, oil and salt and pepper. Cover loosely with foil and roast in a preheated oven, 200°C (400°F), Gas Mark 6, for 20 minutes, until soft. Transfer to a bowl, mash well and set aside until cold.

2 Beat the ricotta and Parmesan into the pumpkin purée and season with salt and pepper to taste.

3 Divide the pasta dough into four pieces and, using a pasta machine, roll out these pieces into long thin strips. Next, cut each strip into 7 x 7.5 cm (3 inch) squares (the size does not have to be exact as they can be trimmed after filling). Take spoonfuls of the filling and set them in the middle of each square. Dampen the edges and fold diagonally in half, forming triangles. Trim the pasta to neaten the parcels and transfer to a floured tea towel (at this stage the parcels may be frozen and can then be cooked straight from the freezer; simply increase the cooking time to about 5 minutes).

4 To make the sauce, melt the butter with the sage and pepper until it just begins to turn a nutty brown colour. Set aside and keep warm.

5 Meanwhile, bring a large saucepan of lightly salted water to a rolling boil, add the pasta triangles, return to the boil and cook for 2–3 minutes. Serve the pasta bathed in the sage butter, with a squeeze of lemon juice and a sprinkling of extra Parmesan.

Serves 4

250 g (8 oz) pumpkin flesh, cubed

1 garlic clove, crushed

2 sage sprigs

2 tablespoons extra virgin olive oil

75 g (3 oz) ricotta cheese

25 g (1 oz) Parmesan cheese, freshly grated

½ quantity Basic Pasta Dough (see page 142)

salt and pepper

Sauce:

75 g (3 oz) butter

2 tablespoons chopped sage

pepper

To serve:

lemon juice

freshly grated Parmesan cheese

spanish pasta with mussels

spain

The Spanish cook several types of pasta dishes and this particular dish, which comes from Catalonia, uses thin short lengths of pasta called fideus. *It was the Moors who first introduced pasta into Catalonia and it differs from Italian pasta in its cooking method. It is never eaten al dente but is cooked until really soft, often in a saffron-infused seafood broth. If you are unable to find* fideus, *use* capellini *and break it into 5 cm (2 inch) lengths.*

500 g (1 lb) monkfish tail

4 tablespoons olive oil

1 onion, finely chopped

4 garlic cloves, finely chopped

500 g (1 lb) ripe tomatoes, skinned, deseeded and chopped

¼ teaspoon saffron threads

1.8 litres (3 pints) Fish Stock (see page 139)

375 g (12 oz) dried fideus or capellini

1 kg (2 lb) small mussels, scrubbed

salt and pepper

Aïoli (see page 134), to serve

1 Wash and dry the monkfish tail and, using a sharp knife, cut through the bone to produce large chunks.

2 Heat half of the oil in a saucepan and fry the onion, garlic and tomatoes for 10 minutes. Add the monkfish, saffron threads and fish stock, bring to the boil and simmer gently for 5 minutes, then remove the fish and set aside. Continue to simmer gently for a further 25 minutes.

3 Meanwhile, heat the remaining oil in a flameproof casserole. Break the pasta into short lengths, add them to the hot oil and fry gently for 5 minutes, stirring constantly, until the pasta is golden.

4 Gradually stir in the tomato broth and simmer gently, stirring, until the pasta is cooked. Add the mussels, stir well and then add the monkfish. Cook for a further 5–6 minutes until the mussels have opened and the monkfish is cooked through. Season with salt and pepper to taste and serve with the aïoli.

Serves 4–6

orzo pilaf with beans & mint

italy

This is a slightly unusual pilaf using orzo, a tiny rice-shaped pasta, sometimes called risi, *with lots of fresh mint. It is available from Italian delicatessens and is excellent served with Gambas a la Plancha (see page 65).*

1 Heat the oil in a large frying pan and fry the onion, leeks, garlic, cumin and saffron for 10 minutes, until the vegetables are softened but not browned.

2 Add the orzo and stir-fry for 1 minute, until all the grains are glossy. Add the mint sprigs and stock and bring to the boil. Cover and simmer for 15–20 minutes, until the orzo is cooked and most of the the liquid has been absorbed.

3 Meanwhile, blanch the beans in lightly salted boiling water for 3–4 minutes until al dente. Drain well.

4 Stir the beans into the orzo with the pine nuts, mint, butter and season with salt and pepper. Cover and cook over a very low heat for 10 minutes. Remove from the heat but leave undisturbed for a further 10 minutes before serving.

Serves 4

4 tablespoons olive oil

1 onion, finely chopped

2 leeks, sliced

2 garlic cloves, crushed

½ teaspoon ground cumin

pinch of saffron threads

375 g (12 oz) orzo

2 mint sprigs

300 ml (½ pint) vegetable stock

250 g (8 oz) French beans

50 g (2 oz) pine nuts, toasted and chopped

4 tablespoons chopped mint

25 g (1 oz) butter

salt and pepper

butter beans in tomato sauce

greece

1 Drain and rinse the beans, place them in a large saucepan and cover generously with cold water. Bring to the boil and then simmer for 1¼–1½ hours, until they are starting to feel tender.

2 Strain the beans, reserving the cooking liquid. Place the beans in a casserole with the oil, onion, garlic, chilli flakes, tomatoes, tomato purée, oregano and season with salt and pepper.

3 Add enough of the reserved liquid to cover the beans, then bake, covered, in a preheated oven, 150°C (300°F), Gas Mark 2, for 1½ hours. Remove the lid and cook for a further 30–45 minutes, until the liquid is reduced and thickened. Serve the beans drizzled with oil and sprinkled with some more oregano.

Serves 4

250 g (8 oz) dried butter beans, soaked overnight in cold water

3 tablespoons olive oil

1 small onion, finely chopped

2 garlic cloves, crushed

¼ teaspoon dried chilli flakes

½ x 400 g (13 oz) can chopped tomatoes

1 tablespoon tomato purée

1 tablespoon dried oregano, plus extra to serve

salt and pepper

extra virgin olive oil, to serve

socca with parmesan

france

Socca is a snack similar to a crêpe, usually eaten mid morning, and is cooked on street stalls throughout Provence. Traditionally socca would be cooked as a thin pancake on a large flat griddle, but here it is first fried in a nonstick frying pan and then grilled to brown the top. The Parmesan is not authentic but it is totally delicious.

1 Sift the chickpea flour into a bowl and stir in the salt and cayenne. Whisk in the water in a steady stream, beating well to avoid lumps. Leave to stand for 30 minutes.

2 Heat half of the oil in a large nonstick frying pan. When the oil is hot, pour in the batter and cook over a moderate heat for 3–4 minutes, until large bubbles begin to appear on the surface.

3 While the socca is cooking, heat the grill. As soon as the socca looks to be set, drizzle over the remaining oil, sprinkle with sea salt and grill as close to the heat source as possible, being careful not to burn the handle of the pan. Cook for 3–4 minutes, until the top is starting to brown in spots, remove from the heat and immediately sprinkle over the Parmesan. Cool slightly and serve cut into wedges.

Serves 4

75 g (3 oz) chickpea flour

½ teaspoon sea salt, plus extra to sprinkle

a good pinch of cayenne pepper

250 ml (8 fl oz) water

2 tablespoons olive oil

a little freshly grated Parmesan cheese, to serve

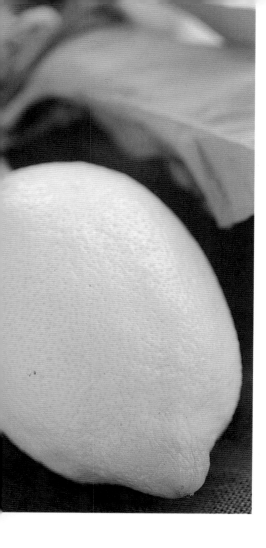

lemon, leek & bay leaf risotto

italy

The addition of bay to this lemon risotto is not actually authentic, but I love the flavour it gives. This dish is a good accompaniment to grilled fish or shellfish.

1 Melt the butter in a deep frying pan and fry the onion, garlic and leeks for 10 minutes, until softened, but not browned. Add the rice and bay leaves and stir for 1 minute, until the grains are coated and glossy. Add the vermouth and reduce by half.

2 Meanwhile, heat the stock in a saucepan to a very gentle simmer. Gradually add the stock to the rice, a ladleful at a time, stirring constantly until the rice is tender, but still al dente.

3 Add the lemon juice and rind and some salt and pepper and stir for a further 5 minutes. Add the mascarpone and Parmesan, stir once, cover and leave the risotto to rest for a few minutes. Serve with grated Parmesan.

Serves 4

50 g (2 oz) butter

1 onion, finely chopped

2 garlic cloves, crushed

2 leeks, trimmed, washed and sliced

250 g (8 oz) risotto rice

6 bay leaves, bruised

150 ml (¼ pint) dry vermouth

1–1.2 litres (1¾–2 pints) Chicken Stock (see page 139) or vegetable stock

juice and rind of 1 large unwaxed lemon

50 g (2 oz) mascarpone cheese

50 g (2 oz) Parmesan cheese, freshly grated, plus extra for serving

salt and pepper

pea & prawn risotto

italy

500 g (1 lb) raw prawns

125 g (4 oz) butter

1 onion, finely chopped

2 garlic cloves, crushed

250 g (8 oz) risotto rice

375 g (12 oz) shelled peas

150 ml (¼ pint) dry white wine

1.5 litres (2½ pints) vegetable stock

4 tablespoons chopped mint

salt and pepper

A classic combination of fresh peas and prawns make a delightful addition to a creamy risotto. It is important to remember that the Italians never add Parmesan to a dish that contains seafood.

1 Peel the prawns, reserving the heads and shells. Devein each prawn, wash and pat dry. Wash the heads and shells and dry well.

2 Melt half of the butter in a large frying pan, add the heads and shells and stir-fry for 3–4 minutes, until golden. Strain the butter and return it to the pan.

3 Add a further 25 g (1 oz) of the butter to the pan and gently fry the onion and garlic for 5 minutes until softened. Add the rice and stir the grains for 1 minute, until coated and glossy. Add the peas and then pour in the wine and boil rapidly until reduced by half.

4 Meanwhile, bring the stock to a very gentle simmer in another pan and start adding it to the rice, a ladleful at a time. Stir constantly while gradually adding the stock until the rice is creamy but still crunchy in the middle and most of the liquid has been absorbed. This takes about 20 minutes.

5 Melt the remaining butter and stir-fry the prawns for 3–4 minutes, then stir them into the rice with the pan juices, mint and season with salt and pepper to taste. Cover the pan and leave to rest for 5 minutes. Serve hot.

Serves 6

black rice with squid

spain

This dish of rice and squid cooked in their own ink is enormously popular throughout Spain and can be found on menus in many seafood restaurants. Fortunately, today it is not necessary to remove the ink sacs from each individual squid (a time-consuming and tiresome job) as small sachets of squid ink are available from most good fishmongers. Two sachets will be sufficient for this recipe.

1 Melt half of the butter and stir-fry the squid for 3–4 minutes, until lightly golden. Stir in the remaining butter, add the onion, garlic and tomatoes and fry gently for 5 minutes.

2 Add the rice and stir for 1 minute, until the grains are coated and glossy. Pour in the wine and boil until reduced by half.

3 Stir in the squid ink and all the stock and season lightly with salt and pepper. Bring to the boil and simmer gently, uncovered, for 15–20 minutes, until the rice is tender. Do not stir. Remove the pan from the heat, cover and leave to rest for 4–5 minutes. Taste and adjust the seasoning, if necessary and serve hot.

Serves 4

50 g (2 oz) butter

400 g (13 oz) small squid, cleaned and diced

1 large onion, finely chopped

4 garlic cloves, crushed

2 ripe tomatoes, skinned, deseeded and chopped

250 g (8 oz) Spanish short-grain rice (or risotto rice)

150 ml (¼ pint) dry white wine

2 sachets squid ink (see left)

600 ml (1 pint) Fish Stock (see page 139)

salt and pepper

chickpea & rice pilaf

turkey

Pilafs are popular throughout the Middle East and North Africa. The staple ingredient used in a pilaf varies – it can be rice, bulgar wheat, couscous or chickpeas. This recipe combines chickpeas and rice in a richly spiced dish.

1 Drain the chickpeas, place in a saucepan and cover with plenty of cold water. Bring to the boil and simmer, uncovered, for 1–1½ hours, until tender. Drain the chickpeas, reserving 4 tablespoons of the cooking liquid, and set aside.

2 Cook the rice until just tender, according to packet instructions, drain and set aside.

3 Heat the oil in a large frying pan and fry half of the onions, the garlic, leek and chilli for 10 minutes, until softened and lightly browned. Add the salt, pepper, spices, tomatoes, lemon juice and the reserved chickpea liquid, cover and simmer gently for 15 minutes.

4 Stir in the chickpeas and rice and heat through for 5 minutes. Remove from the heat but leave undisturbed for a further 10 minutes.

5 Meanwhile, melt the butter and fry the remaining onions until golden and slightly crispy. Stir into the pilaf with the herbs and serve immediately.

Serves 6

125 g (4 oz) dried chickpeas, soaked overnight

250 g (8 oz) brown rice

4 tablespoons extra virgin olive oil

2 onions, sliced

1 garlic clove, finely chopped

1 leek, sliced

1 red chilli, deseeded and chopped

1 teaspoon salt

½ teaspoon pepper

½ teaspoon each ground coriander, cumin and cinnamon

4 plum tomatoes, diced

juice of ½ lemon

25 g (1 oz) butter

2 tablespoons each chopped parsley and coriander

fruit & nut couscous with chicken skewers

morocco

A pilaf, with couscous as the staple ingredient, suggests that the origin of a recipe could be Moroccan. This dish, which is a meal in itself was inspired by the cooking and flavours of North Africa.

1 Cut the chicken into long thin strips, place them in a shallow dish and add the olive oil, garlic, spices and lemon juice. Stir well then cover and leave to marinate for 2 hours. Thread the chicken strips on to 8 small, presoaked wooden skewers.

2 To prepare the couscous, heat half of the oil in a saucepan and fry the onion, garlic and spices for 5 minutes. Stir in the dried fruits and almonds and remove from the heat.

3 Meanwhile, pour the stock over the couscous, cover with a tea towel and steam for 8–10 minutes, until the grains are fluffed up and the liquid absorbed. Stir in the remaining oil, fruit and nut mixture, add the lemon juice and coriander and season with salt and pepper to taste.

4 While the couscous is steaming, griddle or grill the chicken skewers for 4–5 minutes on each side, until charred and cooked through. Serve with the couscous, garnished with pomegranate seeds, lemon wedges and coriander sprigs.

Serves 4

500 g (1 lb) free range skinless chicken breast fillets

2 tablespoons extra virgin olive oil

2 garlic cloves, crushed

½ teaspoon each ground cumin, turmeric and paprika

2 teaspoons lemon juice

Couscous:

4 tablespoons extra virgin olive oil

1 small onion, finely chopped

1 garlic clove, crushed

1 teaspoon each ground cumin, cinnamon, pepper and ginger

50 g (2 oz) dried dates, chopped

50 g (2 oz) dried apricots, finely chopped

50 g (2 oz) blanched almonds, toasted and chopped

600 ml (1 pint) vegetable stock

175 g (6 oz) couscous

1 tablespoon lemon juice

2 tablespoons chopped coriander

salt and pepper

To garnish:

seeds from half a pomegranate

lemon wedges

coriander sprigs

savoury bakes

Outdoor ovens were introduced to the Mediterranean by the Romans as long ago as the second century BC, and with them came classic dishes such as pizzas and pies. Originally the ovens were communal, with just one large oven serving each village. These ovens are still used in many places today. Breads of all types are popular, from the unleavened varieties of Turkey and the Middle East to olive breads and the sourdoughs of Spain and France.

eliotes

cyprus

2½ teaspoons dried active yeast

300 ml (½ pint) warmed water

1 teaspoon caster sugar

500 g (1 lb) strong white flour

125 g (4 oz) wholemeal flour

2 teaspoons each dried mint and oregano

1½ teaspoons sea salt, plus extra to sprinkle

3 tablespoons extra virgin olive oil, plus extra to drizzle

175 g (6 oz) kalamata olives, pitted

For many years now I have lived on the edges of a large Turkish Cypriot community and one of my favourite treats is a bag of freshly made olive rolls, still warm, to munch as I make my way home. This is my version.

1 Dissolve the yeast in the warmed water, stir in the sugar and leave to froth in a warm place for 10 minutes.

2 Sift the flour into the bowl of a food mixer and stir in the herbs and salt. Gradually work in the frothed yeast mixture and oil to form a soft dough, adding a little extra warm water, if necessary. Knead for 8–10 minutes until the dough is smooth and elastic.

3 Finely chop 25 g (1 oz) of the pitted olives and slice the rest. Transfer the dough to a lightly floured surface and work in the chopped olives until evenly incorporated. Shape into a ball, place in an oiled bowl, cover with oiled plastic and leave to rise for at least 1 hour until doubled in size.

4 Knock back the dough, divide into 8 and shape each one into a flat round. Place a spoonful of the remaining olives in the centre of the dough, pull up and pinch the edges together to seal and shape into rolls.

5 Place the rolls seam side down on two greased baking sheets, cover with oiled plastic and leave to rise for a further 30–45 minutes until doubled in size. Drizzle the rolls with a little oil, sprinkle over some sea salt and bake in a preheated oven, 220°C (425°F), Gas Mark 7, for 20–25 minutes, until risen and golden. Cool on a wire rack and eat whilst still warm.

Makes 8

pissaladière

france

1 quantity Basic Pizza Dough
(see page 143)

25 g (1 oz) butter

1 kg (2 lb) large onions, thinly sliced

2 garlic cloves, crushed

1 tablespoon chopped thyme

1 teaspoon dried oregano

2 tablespoons salted capers,
washed and dried

6 salted anchovies, washed
and chopped

a few Niçoise olives

salt and pepper

crème fraîche or goat's cheese,
such as Provençal banon, to serve

Italy has pizzas; Provence has the pissaladière, which originated in Nice. It is topped with caramelized onions, anchovy fillets and olives. Like many dishes, there is no definitive recipe; some people suggest a pastry case, others a pizza dough; some versions are made with a tomato paste spread over the base, while others contain cream and eggs like a flan. This recipe uses a pizza dough.

1 Make up the pizza dough and set aside to rise for 1 hour. Divide the dough in half. Wrap one piece in oiled clingfilm and freeze for later use.

2 Meanwhile, melt the butter in a large frying pan and fry the onions, garlic, thyme and oregano for 25 minutes, until golden and caramelized. Season with salt and pepper to taste, remove from the heat and leave to cool.

3 Place a large baking sheet in a preheated oven, 230°C (450°F), Gas Mark 8, to heat up. Roll out the risen dough on a lightly floured surface to form a 33 cm (13 inch) round, prick the base and transfer to a second baking sheet.

4 Spread over the onion mixture, dot with the capers, anchovies and olives and place on the heated sheet in the oven. Bake for 15–20 minutes, until the base is cooked through. Serve at room temperature with some goat's cheese or crème fraîche.

Serves 2–4

griddle bread

turkey

500 g (1 lb) plain flour

250 g (8 oz) wholemeal flour

2 teaspoons salt

1 teaspoon fast-acting yeast

450 ml (¾ pint) warm water

1 tablespoon extra virgin olive oil,
plus extra for brushing

1 Sift the flours and salt into the bowl of a food mixer. Stir in the yeast and then, with the dough hook turning, gradually add the water and oil to form a soft dough. Knead for 8–10 minutes, until smooth and elastic.

2 Transfer the dough to an oiled bowl, cover with a tea towel and leave to rise in a warm place for 1 hour, until doubled in size.

3 Divide the dough into eight pieces and roll out each one on a lightly floured surface to form an oval (about the same size as commercial pitta breads), brush with a little oil and leave to rise for about 10 minutes.

4 Heat a griddle or heavy-based pan until really hot and cook the breads for about 2 minutes on each side, until spotted with brown and puffed up. Serve immediately.

Serves 8

pizza margherita

italy

This is perhaps the most basic of pizza toppings, but I have included it for two reasons. First, simple or not, I love it. Next, it is easily adaptable; you can add all sorts of other ingredients of your choice, such as capers, anchovies, tuna or roast vegetables.

1 Prepare the pizza dough.

2 To make the topping, place the tomato flesh in a bowl and stir in the basil, garlic, oregano, chilli flakes and olive oil. Cover and leave to marinate for 30 minutes.

3 Heat the oven to 240°C (475°F), Gas Mark 9 and place a baking sheet or pizza stone on the middle shelf to heat up.

4 Divide the dough into four pieces and roll one piece out thinly on a floured surface to form a 23 cm (9 inch) round. Transfer to a well-floured board or second baking sheet and top with a quarter of the tomato salsa, a quarter of the mozzarella and a quarter of the Parmesan and season with salt and pepper to taste.

5 Carefully slide the pizza straight on to the heated baking sheet and bake for about 10–12 minutes, until the base is cooked and the topping is bubbling.

6 Prepare the second pizza while the first one is cooking and so on with all four. Eat the pizzas immediately they are ready.

Serves 4

Variation: Divide the dough in half and roll out to 33 cm (13 inch) rounds, top and bake for 15–18 minutes. Each pizza serves 2.

1 quantity Basic Pizza Dough (see page 143)

Topping:

500 g (1 lb) ripe plum tomatoes, skinned, deseeded and diced

2 tablespoons chopped basil

2 garlic cloves, crushed

½ teaspoon dried oregano

pinch of dried chilli flakes

1 tablespoon olive oil

300 g (10 oz) mozzarella cheese, grated

25 g (1 oz) Parmesan cheese, freshly grated

salt and pepper

roast onion, gorgonzola & walnut pizza

italy

1 quantity Basic Pizza Dough (see page 143)

a little dressed rocket, to garnish (optional)

Topping:

3 red onions

2 tablespoons extra virgin olive oil, plus extra to drizzle

2 tablespoons chopped sage

1 tablespoon balsamic vinegar

175 g (6 oz) Gorgonzola cheese, crumbled

4 tablespoons crème fraîche

45 g (1½ oz) shelled walnuts, roughly chopped

pepper

Here, the sweetness of the roast onions is balanced perfectly by the tartness of Gorgonzola while the addition of walnuts adds a surprisingly pleasant bite. When making pizzas, it is essential that they are eaten as soon as they are cooked, so if you only have one oven you must cook the pizzas one at a time and eat them in stages.

1 While the pizza dough is rising prepare the topping. Cut each onion into eight wedges, place them in a shallow roasting dish and drizzle over the oil. Top with half of the sage and season well with salt and pepper. Roast in a preheated oven, 220°C (425°F), Gas Mark 7, for 20–30 minutes until soft and caramelized. Add the vinegar and cook for a further 5 minutes. Leave to cool.

2 Increase the oven temperature to 240°C (475°F), Gas Mark 9 and place a large baking sheet on the middle shelf. Cream together the Gorgonzola and crème fraîche.

3 Divide the pizza dough into four and roll out one piece on a floured surface to form a thin 23 cm (9 inch) round. Transfer to a well floured board or second baking sheet and top with quarter each of the onions, cheese mixture, the remaining sage and walnuts. Season with pepper and drizzle with a little olive oil.

4 Carefully slide the pizza on to the heated baking sheet. Bake for 10–12 minutes until the base is crisp and the topping melted. Prepare the second pizza while the first one is cooking and so on with all four.

5 Serve the pizzas garnished with a little rocket, if liked.

Serves 4

Variation: Divide the dough in half and roll out to two 33 cm (14 inch) rounds. Add the topping and bake for 15–18 minutes. Each pizza serves 2.

sourdough with semolina

spain

Starter dough:

280 ml (8 fl oz) warm water

¼ teaspoon dry active yeast

375 g (12 oz) strong white flour

½ teaspoon sugar

Bread dough:

1¼ teaspoons dry active yeast

900 ml (1½ pints) warm water

1 teaspoon sugar

750 g (1½ lb) strong white flour

**250 g (8 oz) semolina, extra
for sprinkling**

1½ tablespoons salt

*This dough will be very wet, but this is correct. It is hardly kneaded at all, just stirred together
and left to rise. You will need to flour the surface well, before turning over the dough.*

1 Four days before making the bread, prepare the starter dough. Put the warm water
into a small bowl and stir in the yeast to dissolve it. Add about 4 tablespoons of the flour
and the sugar and leave to froth in a warm place for 10 minutes. Work the mixture into
the remaining flour, cover with clingfilm and leave in a warm place for at least 3 days.

2 To begin the bread dough, dissolve the yeast in 150 ml (¼ pint) of the warm water, add
the sugar and 4 tablespoons of the flour and froth for 10 minutes. Transfer to a large bowl
and gradually work in 125 g (4 oz) of the starter dough (refrigerate the rest and use as
required), the remaining warm water, the remaining flour, the semolina and salt until a
quite sticky, slightly lumpy dough forms.

3 Transfer the dough to an oiled bowl, cover with oiled plastic and leave in a warm place
for several hours to double in size.

4 Carefully tip out the dough on to a floured surface, cut off about 125 g (4 oz) and add it
to the starter dough mixture. Cut the remaining dough in half and shape each piece into a
flat round. Roll the dough up, turn it 180° and repeat the rolling. Transfer to a well-floured
baking sheet, sprinkle the surface with semolina and cover with a clean tea towel.

5 Leave the dough to rise for 1–2 hours, until doubled. Score the surface with a sharp
knife and bake in a preheated oven, 230°C (450°F), Gas Mark 8, for 30 minutes. Cool on a
wire rack.

Makes 2 round loaves

chicken & sweet potato filo pie

morocco

This is a bisteeya, *the traditional Moroccan pastry pie. You will need to buy large sheets of filo pastry which are widely available from specialist food stores, Middle Eastern shops and some supermarkets.*

1 Place the chicken in a saucepan with the onion, garlic, ginger, cinnamon sticks, chilli, turmeric, saffron, coriander sprigs and 1 teaspoon each of salt and pepper. Add just enough water to cover the chicken, bring it to the boil and simmer gently for about 45 minutes–1 hour until the chicken is cooked.

2 Meanwhile, steam the sweet potatoes for 10–15 minutes, until tender.

3 Carefully remove the chicken from the pan and, as soon as it is cool enough to handle, cut away and shred the meat, discarding the skin.

4 Remove the cinnamon sticks and boil the stock rapidly for about 40–45 minutes, until about 300 ml (½ pint) liquid remains and the onion mixture is sticky. Strain and reserve the liquid, leaving the onion mixture in the pan.

5 Combine the eggs and lemon juice and stir into the pan. Cook over a low heat until the mixture is dry and curdled in appearance.

6 Heat 25 g (1 oz) of the butter and gently fry the almonds until golden, being careful not to burn the butter. Transfer the almonds to a food processor with the pan juices and process briefly with the icing sugar.

7 Melt the remaining butter. Lay two sheets of pastry on the work surface to form a 35 cm (14 inch) square and brush with butter. Brush the remaining four sheets with butter and place on top to give three layers in total. Press into an oiled 30 cm (12 inch) loose-based cake tin, allowing the sheets to overhang the edge.

8 In a large bowl, combine all the filling ingredients and season with salt and pepper to taste. Spoon into the tin, drawing the overhanging edges over the filling to enclose it. Brush the pie with the remaining butter, transfer to a preheated oven, 200°C (400°F), Gas Mark 6, and bake for 30 minutes, until golden. Reheat the reserved reduced stock and keep warm.

9 Dust the pie with a mixture of ground cinnamon and icing sugar and serve in wedges drizzled with a little of the stock.

Serves 6

1.5 kg (3 lb) free-range chicken

1 onion, chopped

4 garlic cloves, peeled but left whole

2 teaspoons grated fresh root ginger

2 cinnamon sticks

1 red chilli, deseeded and chopped

1 teaspoon ground turmeric

¼ teaspoon saffron threads

4 coriander sprigs

500 g (1 lb) sweet potatoes, cubed

4 eggs, lightly beaten

2 tablespoons lemon juice

125 g (4 oz) butter

175 g (6 oz) blanched almonds

2 tablespoons icing sugar

6 large sheets filo pastry (see page 8)

salt and pepper

icing sugar mixed with a little ground cinnamon, to serve

piadini with chilli prawns & salsa verde

italy

Italian flat breads, similar to Mexican tortillas, piadini *are served as a base for various toppings in a similar way to* bruschetta *and* crostini. *They are cooked on a griddle.*

1 Sift the flour and salt into a bowl, make a well in the centre and work in the oil and water to form a soft dough. Knead on a lightly floured surface until smooth, wrap in clingfilm and leave to rest for 30 minutes.

2 Meanwhile, peel and devein the prawns. Wash and dry well.

3 Divide the dough into four pieces and roll each one out on a lightly floured surface to form an 18 cm (7 inch) round.

4 Heat a griddle or heavy-based frying pan until really hot. Fry the piadini, one at a time, for 1 minute, until bubbling up and golden underneath, flip over and cook on the second side for a further 30 seconds. Keep warm in a low oven while cooking the rest.

5 To make the topping, heat the olive oil in a frying pan, add the prawns and stir-fry for 3–4 minutes. Add the garlic and chilli, and cook for a further 1–2 minutes until the prawns are cooked through. Add a squeeze of lemon juice, season with salt and pepper and divide the prawns between the piadini, topping each one with a spoonful of salsa or pesto. Garnish with chives and basil leaves and serve immediately.

Serves 4

125 g (4 oz) plain flour
¼ teaspoon salt
1 tablespoon olive oil
65 ml (2½ fl oz) tepid water
Salsa Verde (see page 136)
or Pesto (see page 138), to serve

Topping:
16 large raw prawns
2 tablespoons extra virgin olive oil
1 garlic clove, sliced
½ teaspoon dried chilli flakes
squeeze of lemon juice
salt and pepper

To garnish:
chives
basil leaves

desserts

The Mediterranean people share a love of all things sweet, but they are not necessarily eaten as desserts – a meal will often end with a plate of fresh fruit, served in slices straight from the refrigerator. Many sweets are made to eat as a snack, such as the small filo pastries of Greece and Turkey. Egg custards are common in Spain while the Italians are famous for their wide variety of rich ices and sorbets.

chocolate & rosemary ice cream

italy

600 ml (1 pint) double cream

150 ml (¼ pint) milk

seeds from 1 vanilla pod

4 rosemary sprigs, bruised, plus extra, to garnish

5 egg yolks

125 g (4 oz) caster sugar

125 g (4 oz) dark chocolate, grated

Italians are passionate about ice cream and this rich chocolate gelato is infused with the aromatic herb rosemary to add an exotic flavour. Although it may seem a strange combination, the two flavours go together really well.

1 Warm the cream, milk, vanilla seeds and rosemary sprigs in a saucepan until almost boiling. Remove from the heat and leave to infuse for 10 minutes. Pick out the rosemary sprigs and reserve.

2 Beat the egg yolks and sugar until pale and then carefully beat in the cream mixture. Strain back into the saucepan and heat gently, stirring constantly, until the custard thickens enough to coat the back of a wooden spoon. Do not allow the custard to boil.

3 Remove the custard from the heat and immediately stir in the chocolate and continue to stir until it is melted. Transfer to a plastic container, add the rosemary sprigs and leave until completely cold. Discard the rosemary.

4 Freeze the ice cream either in an ice cream maker, following the manufacturer's instructions, or in the freezer, beating the ice cream after an hour or so to break down any ice crystals. Remove from the freezer 15–20 minutes before serving to soften slightly. Garnish with rosemary sprigs.

Serves 4

walnut cake with coffee syrup

greece

6 eggs, separated

125 g (4 oz) clear honey

50 g (2 oz) caster sugar

250 g (8 oz) shelled walnuts, toasted and ground

50 g (2 oz) plain flour

1 teaspoon baking powder

2 teaspoons ground cinnamon

Coffee syrup:

300 ml (½ pint) strong fresh coffee

125 g (4 oz) caster sugar

To serve:

Greek yogurt

clear honey

It is usual in Greece to serve this type of walnut cake soaked in a honey syrup. This version with a coffee-flavoured syrup is not authentically Greek, but the syrup adds a delicious and unique flavour.

1 Grease and base-line a 23 cm (9 inch) springform tin. Beat the egg yolks, honey and sugar until pale and creamy. Mix together the walnuts, flour, baking powder and cinnamon and stir into the creamed mixture.

2 Whisk the egg whites until stiff, stir 1 tablespoon into the cake mixture and then fold in the rest until evenly incorporated. Spoon into the prepared tin and bake in a preheated oven, 180°C (350°F), Gas Mark 4, for 30 minutes until the cake has risen and shrunk slightly from the sides of the tin.

3 Meanwhile, heat the coffee in a small pan with the sugar, stirring until the sugar has dissolved. Boil for 3–4 minutes, until syrupy.

4 Leave the cake to cool in the tin for 5 minutes, then transfer it to a large plate. Spike all over with a skewer and drizzle over the syrup. Leave until completely cold and serve in wedges with Greek yogurt and drizzled with honey.

Serves 8

orange and almond torte

spain

This torte is based on the classic Spanish cake, tarta de naranja. *After cooking, the light almond sponge cake is cooled and then soaked with an aromatic orange and cardamom syrup. The addition of the spice shows the Moorish influence, typical of many Spanish dishes.*

1 Grease and base-line a 23 cm (9 inch) springform cake tin, then dust lightly with flour. In a mixing bowl, beat the egg yolks, sugar and orange rind and juice until pale and then stir in the almonds and breadcrumbs. The mixture at this stage is quite thick.

2 Whisk the egg whites until just stiff. Stir a spoonful into the cake mixture and then carefully fold in the rest until evenly incorporated. Transfer to the prepared tin and bake in a preheated oven, 180°C (350°F), Gas Mark 4, for 35–40 minutes, until risen and springy to the touch. Leave the torte to cool in the tin for 5 minutes, then transfer to a wire rack to cool completely.

3 To make the syrup, warm the orange juice, cardamom and sugar in a small saucepan until the sugar has dissolved, then boil for 3 minutes, until syrupy. Spike the cake all over with a skewer and pour over the syrup. Serve the torte in wedges with crème fraîche or whipped cream.

Serves 8

6 eggs, separated
175 g (6 oz) caster sugar
grated rind and juice of 1 orange
175 g (6 oz) ground almonds
75 g (3 oz) day-old breadcrumbs
flour, for dusting
crème fraîche or whipped cream, to serve

Syrup:
juice of 3 oranges
3 cardamom pods, bruised
50 g (2 oz) caster sugar

fragrant orange salad with dates

tunisia

1 Squeeze the juice from 1 of the oranges into a bowl and stir in the lemon juice, orange flower water, icing sugar and cinnamon.

2 Peel the remaining oranges and slice them thinly, working over the bowl of dressing, to catch any juices.

3 Arrange the orange slices on a large plate. Scoop out the seeds from the pomegranate and scatter over the oranges with the date slices. Pour over the dressing and serve the salad dusted with a little icing sugar and ground cinnamon.

Serves 4

7 oranges
juice of 1 lemon
2 tablespoons orange flower water
1 tablespoon icing sugar, plus extra to serve
1 teaspoon ground cinnamon, plus extra to serve
½ pomegranate
125 g (4 oz) medjool dates, pitted and sliced

panna cotta with blueberry compôte

italy

This Italian custard pudding flavoured with vanilla should contain just enough gelatine to set it but leave the texture still a little wobbly. The blueberry compôte is not particularly Italian but it complements the pudding beautifully. Amaretto di Saronno is an Italian almond liqueur.

1 Heat 450 ml (¾ pint) of the cream in a saucepan with the vanilla seeds, lemon rind and sugar until it almost reaches boiling point, then strain through a fine sieve.

2 Soak the gelatine in the liqueur for 1 minute, then heat very gently until the gelatine dissolves. It is important that the gelatine does not boil, as this destabilizes it. Stir a little of the vanilla cream into the pan and then pour this back into the rest of the vanilla cream.

3 Whisk the remaining cream until it forms soft peaks and fold it into the cooled vanilla cream. Pour into eight 150 ml (¼ pint) moulds and chill for 2–3 hours, until set.

4 Meanwhile, place the blueberries, sugar, lemon juice and water in a saucepan and heat gently until the blueberries soften and the liquid becomes a little syrupy. Leave to cool.

5 Unmould the set panna cotta by briefly immersing the base and sides of the moulds in hot water. Invert on to plates and spoon the blueberry compôte around them.

Serves 8

600 ml (1 pint) double cream
1 vanilla pod, split lengthways
4 strips of lemon rind
50 g (2 oz) caster sugar
1½ teaspoons gelatine
2 tablespoons Amaretto di Saronno liqueur

Blueberry compôte:
250 g (8 oz) blueberries
50 g (2 oz) caster sugar
squeeze of lemon juice
2 tablespoons water

panforte with chocolate & ginger

italy

175 g (6 oz) mixed candied fruit and peel, diced

50 g (2 oz) crystallized ginger, chopped

100 g (3½ oz) blanched almonds

50 g (2 oz) pine nuts

50 g (2 oz) dark chocolate, chopped

50 g (2 oz) plain flour

25 g (1 oz) cocoa powder

1 teaspoon ground cinnamon

½ teaspoon each ground cloves, cardamom and mace

4 tablespoons orange juice

125 g (4 oz) granulated sugar

2 tablespoons clear honey

rice paper, for lining

icing sugar, to decorate

This rich, chewy cake from Sienna is traditionally served at Christmas time. As it is quite a sticky cake, it is baked on a layer of rice paper so that it comes easily out of the tin when it is cooked. It keeps well and can be stored, wrapped in foil, for up to 3 months.

1 Grease a 20 cm (8 inch) loose-based cake tin and line the sides and base with a layer of rice paper.

2 In a mixing bowl, combine the candied fruit and peel, ginger, almonds, pine nuts and chocolate with the flour, cocoa powder and spices.

3 Gently heat the orange juice, sugar and honey in a small heavy-based saucepan to dissolve the sugar, then increase the heat and boil until the liquid reaches 115°F (210°C) on a sugar thermometer. Pour immediately into the dry ingredients, stirring constantly with a wooden spoon (this will be stiff).

4 Transfer the mixture to the prepared tin, smooth the surface with a palette knife and bake in a preheated oven, 180°C (350°F) Gas Mark 4, for 30 minutes, until bubbles appear evenly over the surface.

5 Leave the cake to cool in the tin for 5 minutes, then carefully remove it from the tin and leave to cool completely on a wire rack. When cold, dust with icing sugar and serve in wedges or fingers.

Serves 8–12

lemon tart with strawberries

france

1 Roll out the pastry on a lightly floured surface and use to line a 25 cm (10 inch) fluted flan tin about 2.5 cm (1 inch) deep. Prick the base and chill for 30 minutes.

2 Line the pastry case with baking parchment, fill with baking beans and bake in a preheated oven, 200°C (400°F), Gas Mark 6, for 10 minutes. Remove the parchment and beans and return the pastry case to the oven for a further 10 minutes, until the pastry is crisp and golden. Leave the pastry case to cool and reduce the oven temperature to 150°C (300°F), Gas Mark 2.

3 Beat together all the filling ingredients, pour them into the pastry case and bake for 20–25 minutes, until the filling is just set. Leave the tart to cool completely, dust with icing sugar and serve in wedges with the strawberries.

Serves 8

1 quantity Sweet Shortcrust Pastry (see page 142)

icing sugar, to dust

250 g (8 oz) ripe strawberries, hulled and halved, to serve

Filling:

3 eggs, plus 1 extra yolk

450 ml (¾ pint) double cream

125 g (4 oz) caster sugar

150 ml (¼ pint) lemon juice

pears poached in rosé wine with cassis

france

This is a classic way of poaching pears and always looks beautiful, as the pears absorb the colour of the poaching liquid. The Crème de Cassis adds a lovely depth of flavour to the dish.

1 Put the wine, cassis and sugar into a small deep saucepan and bring slowly to the boil, stirring frequently to dissolve the sugar.

2 Add the lemon and orange rind, lemon juice and spices, return to the boil and carefully slip in the pears, submerging them as much as possible. Simmer gently, turning the pears frequently so they colour evenly, and cook for 20 minutes, until tender.

3 Remove the pears with a slotted spoon and put them into a bowl. Bring the poaching liquid to the boil and boil until reduced by half to give a syrupy liquid. Pour over the pears and set aside to cool. Serve the pears with some crème fraîche or vanilla ice cream.

Serves 4

450 ml (¾ pint) Provençal rosé wine

50 ml (2 fl oz) Crème de Cassis

50 g (2 oz) caster sugar

2 strips each lemon and orange rind

squeeze of lemon juice

2 cinnamon sticks, bruised

4 cloves

4 large dessert pears, peeled but left whole

crème fraîche or vanilla ice cream, to serve

baked quinces

greece

4 small quinces, each about
250 g (8 oz)

125 g (4 oz) clear honey

300 ml (½ pint) red wine

1 vanilla pod, split lengthways

4 cloves

2 star anise

Lemon yogurt:

125 ml (4 fl oz) Greek yogurt

1 tablespoon clear honey

1 teaspoon lemon juice

To be thoroughly authentic this dish, inspired by a meal I had in Athens, would use the Greek dessert wine Mavrodaphne, but this is hard to find outside its native country. Use a full-bodied new world Cabernet Sauvignon instead.

1 Peel and halve the quinces and arrange them, cut side up, in a roasting tin just large enough to hold them in a single layer.

2 Mix together the honey and wine, pour over the quinces and add the vanilla pod, cloves and star anise. Cover the dish with foil and bake in a preheated oven, 190°C (375°F), Gas Mark 5, for 30 minutes.

3 Remove the foil, baste the quinces and bake for a further 45–50 minutes, basting occasionally, until they are cooked and the juices become syrupy.

4 To make the lemon yogurt, mix all the ingredients together. Serve the quinces warm with the yogurt and pan juices.

Serves 4

fried bread with honey and lemon

spain

300 ml (½ pint) milk

50 g (2 oz) clear honey

2 strips of lemon rind

pinch of ground cinnamon

8 large slices of day-old bread, without crusts

2 eggs

vegetable oil, for frying

To serve:

soured cream

clear honey

lemon wedges

A sweet version of French eggy bread, which the Spanish serve as a breakfast dish. However, I prefer it as a dessert as it brings back memories of my mum's bread and butter pudding.

1 Warm the milk, honey, lemon rind and cinnamon in a saucepan until almost boiling. Remove from the heat and leave to cool for 20 minutes.

2 Cut the bread slices in half diagonally to form triangles and dip each piece into the infused milk. Transfer the slices to a wire rack set over a tray and leave them to dry out for 2 hours.

3 Beat the eggs and heat a shallow layer of oil in a frying pan. Dip the bread triangles into the beaten eggs and fry for 1–2 minutes on each side, until golden. Serve with soured cream, a drizzle of honey and a squeeze of lemon juice.

Serves 4

basics

It is often the simple everyday dishes that become part of the culture of a country's cuisine; look at Pesto (see page 138), the basil sauce which is so evocative of Italian cooking. Gradually, the more we cook these recipes, the more they become second nature and can be prepared with confidence. This chapter is a collection of the sauces, stocks and pastries that are used as an integral part of the other dishes that are found elsewhere in the book.

aïoli, allioli or garlic mayonnaise

2–8 garlic cloves (depending on personal taste)

½ teaspoon sea salt

2 egg yolks

1 tablespoon lemon juice

1 teaspoon Dijon mustard

300 ml (½ pint) French extra virgin olive oil (see page 8)

1–2 teaspoons boiling water (optional)

The emulsification of egg yolks, oil, garlic and salt varies slightly from country to country, with Greece and Portugal adding mashed potato or even breadcrumbs to their versions. The recipe given below is a good representation of the basic garlic sauce.

1 Crush the garlic cloves with the sea salt in a mortar or by pounding together on a board with the side of a knife blade. Transfer to a food processor with the egg yolks, lemon juice and mustard and process briefly until pale.

2 With the motor running, add the oil in a steady stream through the feeder funnel until the sauce is emulsified, thick and glossy. You may need to thin it slightly by whisking in a spoonful or two of boiling water. Cover the surface with clingfilm.

3 Use as a dip for vegetables, an accompaniment for grilled shellfish and fish or as a sandwich filling. Aïoli can be kept chilled in the refrigerator for up to 5 days.

Makes about 300 ml (½ pint)

romesco sauce

spain

1 small ancho chilli

1 large garlic clove, crushed

¼ teaspoon dried chilli flakes

40 g (1½ oz) hazelnuts, toasted

25 g (1 oz) blanched almonds, toasted

1 large tomato, skinned, deseeded and chopped

1 tablespoon chopped parsley

1 tablespoon red wine vinegar

100 ml (3½ fl oz) extra virgin olive oil

salt and pepper

A classic romesco sauce is made with a dried Spanish chilli pepper called a nyora, *which is virtually unobtainable outside Spain. Substitute the dried Mexican chilli,* ancho, *available from specialist food stores.*

1 Soak the ancho chilli in warm water for 30 minutes until rehydrated. Drain, pat dry and chop roughly, transfer to a food processor and process with the garlic, chilli flakes, nuts, tomato and parsley to form a rough paste.

2 Blend in the vinegar and enough oil to form a smooth pesto-like paste. Season with salt and pepper to taste. Spoon into a bowl and cover the surface with clingfilm.

3 Serve with grilled seafood, particularly prawns and squid. This sauce can be kept chilled in the refrigerator for up to 4 days.

Makes about 300 ml (½ pint)

anchoïade

france

A Provençal classic, used as a spread. You don't have to use salted anchovies but they are far superior in both taste and texture to those canned in oil.

1 Roughly chop the anchovies and then pound to a paste with all the remaining ingredients in a mortar or spice grinder until fairly smooth. Transfer to a dish and cover the surface with clingfilm.

2 Serve spread on toasted French bread as an appetizer, or stir into a chicken or meat stock to make a sauce to accompany a roast. Anchoïade can be stored in the refrigerator for several days.

Makes 100 ml (3½ fl oz)

25 g (1 oz) salted anchovies, washed and dried

1 garlic clove, crushed

2 tablespoons olive oil

2 teaspoons lemon juice

¼ teaspoon herbes de Provence

pinch of cayenne pepper

pepper

tapenade

france

Another Provençal classic; olives are the main ingredient in this piquant sauce.

1 Pound together the olives, anchovies, garlic, capers and mustard in a mortar or food processor to form a fairly smooth paste. Gradually add the oil to thin the sauce slightly, then add lemon juice and pepper to taste. Transfer to a dish and cover with clingfilm.

2 Serve spread on toasted bread or stirred into vegetable soups. Tapenade can be stored in the refrigerator for up to 5 days.

Makes 100 ml (3½ fl oz)

125 g (4 oz) Niçoise olives, pitted

2 salted anchovies, washed and dried

1 garlic clove, crushed

2 tablespoons salted capers, rinsed and dried

1 teaspoon Dijon mustard

4 tablespoons extra virgin olive oil

squeeze of lemon juice

pepper

salsa rossa

italy

1 large red pepper

1 tablespoon olive oil

1 garlic clove, crushed

2 ripe tomatoes, skinned and
roughly chopped

pinch of dried chilli flakes

1 teaspoon dried oregano

salt and pepper

Salsa rossa is a red pepper sauce with a hint of chilli from Italy.

1 Grill the pepper until charred all over and cool in a plastic bag. Peel off the skin and discard the seeds, reserving any juices, and chop the flesh.

2 Heat the oil in a saucepan and sauté the garlic for 3 minutes. Add the tomatoes, chilli flakes and oregano and simmer gently for 15 minutes. Stir in the chopped pepper and sauté for 5 minutes to cook off the excess liquid.

3 Tip into a food processor and process to make a fairly smooth sauce. Season with salt and pepper to taste and set aside to cool. Salsa rossa can be stored in a screw-top jar in the refrigerator for up to 5 days.

Makes about 150 ml (¼ pint)

salsa verde

italy

25 g (1 oz) parsley leaves

15 g (½ oz) mixed herbs, such as
basil, chives and mint

1 garlic clove, chopped

15 g (½ oz) pitted green olives

1 tablespoon salted capers, rinsed
and dried

2 dried anchovy fillets, washed
and chopped

1 teaspoon Dijon mustard

2 teaspoons white wine vinegar

125 ml (4 fl oz) extra virgin olive oil

salt and pepper

Another Italian speciality, this time a green herb sauce with the piquant flavours of capers and green olives. Both Salsa Rossa and Salsa Verde can be used as pasta sauces and dips for vegetables and are also good served with grilled fish and meat.

1 Place all the ingredients except the oil in a food processor and process to form a smooth paste. Gradually add the oil to form a sauce. Taste and adjust the seasoning. Salsa verde can be stored in the refrigerator in a screw-top jar for up to 5 days.

Makes about 200 ml (7 fl oz)

pesto

italy

50 g (2 oz) basil leaves

1 garlic clove, crushed

2 tablespoons pine nuts

¼ teaspoon sea salt

6–8 tablespoons extra virgin olive oil

2 tablespoons freshly grated Parmesan cheese

pepper

We all know how to make this delicious Italian basil and garlic sauce, but I don't feel any book on Mediterranean cooking is complete without a recipe.

1 Grind the basil, garlic, pine nuts and sea salt in a mortar or food processor to form a fairly smooth paste. Slowly add the oil until you reach the required texture, soft but not runny, and then add the cheese and pepper to taste. Transfer to a bowl and cover the surface with clingfilm.

2 Serve tossed with freshly cooked pasta, spooned on to soups or with grilled fish or chicken. Pesto can be kept chilled for up to 3 days in the refrigerator.

Makes about 150 ml (¼ pint)

Variation: Red Pesto. Add 25 g (1 oz) drained and chopped sun-dried tomatoes in oil to the basil and continue as above, omitting the Parmesan.

french dressing

2 tablespoons red wine vinegar

2 teaspoons Dijon mustard

1 teaspoon caster sugar

150 ml (¼ pint) extra virgin olive oil

salt and pepper

Used to dress salads all over France (and in fact all over the world), this is a classic dressing. You can use white wine vinegar if you prefer or substitute a balsamic vinegar for a more Italian flavour or sherry vinegar for a Spanish one.

1 Place all the ingredients is a screw-top jar and shake well. Taste and adjust the seasoning if necessary. This dressing can be stored in a cool place for up to 1 week.

Makes about 175 ml (6 fl oz)

fish stock

Ask your fishmonger for any trimmings; they are either free or very cheap. When making a fish stock, it is important not to cook the fish trimmings for more than 30 minutes as the fish heads can make the stock bitter.

1 Place all the ingredients in a large saucepan, bring to the boil, cover and simmer gently for 30 minutes. Strain into a clean pan and boil rapidly until reduced and about 900 ml (1½ pints) remain. Cool and then refrigerate until required.

2 This stock will freeze well for up to 3 months.

Makes about 900 ml (1½ pints)

1 kg (2 lb) fish heads and trimmings, washed

900 ml (1½ pints) dry white wine

900 ml (1½ pints) water

2 carrots, sliced

1 onion, chopped

1 leek, sliced

2 celery sticks, sliced

1 garlic clove, peeled but left whole

2 bay leaves

2 parsley sprigs

2 thyme sprigs

6 white peppercorns

1 teaspoon salt

chicken stock

1 Place all the ingredients in a large saucepan and add enough water to cover, about 2.5 litres (4 pints). Bring slowly to the boil, skimming the surface as necessary, and gently simmer for 1 hour. Remove the chicken and strain the broth into a bowl. Cool and refrigerate until required.

2 Once cold, this stock can be frozen for up to 3 months.

Makes about 1.5 litres (2½ pints)

1 kg (2 lb) free-range chicken

2 carrots, roughly chopped

3 celery sticks, roughly chopped

1 onion, chopped

1 leek, chopped

6 garlic cloves

2 tomatoes, roughly chopped

2 bay leaves

2 thyme sprigs

6 white peppercorns

1 teaspoon sea salt

preserved lemons

morocco

4 unwaxed lemons

50 g (2 oz) sea salt

1 teaspoon coriander seeds

1 small cinnamon stick, bruised

2 bay leaves

juice of 1 lemon

Preserved lemons are a vital ingredient in many Moroccan stews, in particular Chicken, Lemon and Olive Stew. They are indispensable for the sharp flavour and soft texture they impart, which is impossible to replicate with any other ingredient. Either make your own or buy ready preserved lemons for an authentic Moroccan flavour.

1 Scald a large, wide-necked jar with boiling water and dry thoroughly. Cut the lemons into six wedges but leave attached at one end, sprinkle some of the salt into the incisions.

2 Sprinkle some of the remaining salt into the bottom of the jar. Layer the lemons, spices, bay leaves and salt in the jar.

3 Add any remaining salt, the lemon juice and enough boiling water to cover the lemons. Seal the jar and leave in a warm place for at least 2 weeks for the fruit to soften. Once opened, the jar should be stored in the refrigerator.

Makes 4

shortcrust pastry

200 g (7 oz) plain flour, sifted
½ teaspoon salt
125 g (4 oz) chilled butter, diced
3–4 tablespoons cold water

1 Place the flour and salt in a bowl and rub in the butter until the mixture resembles fine breadcrumbs. Gradually work in the water to form a soft dough.

2 Knead lightly on a floured surface and form into a ball. Wrap in clingfilm and chill for 30 minutes.

Makes one 25 cm (10 inch) tart case

sweet shortcrust pastry

200 g (7 oz) plain flour
½ teaspoon salt
100 g (3½ oz) chilled butter, diced
2 tablespoons icing sugar
2 egg yolks
1–2 teaspoons cold water (optional)

1 Sift the flour into a bowl, add the salt and then rub in the butter until the mixture resembles breadcrumbs.

2 Stir in the sugar and then gradually work in the egg yolks to form a soft dough, adding a little cold water if necessary. Knead on a lightly floured surface, wrap in clingfilm and chill for 30 minutes.

Makes one 25 cm (10 inch) tart case

basic pasta dough

250 g (8 oz) pasta flour, plus extra for dusting
3 teaspoons salt
2 eggs, plus 1 egg yolk
1 tablespoons extra virgin olive oil
1–2 tablespoons cold water

1 Sift the flour and 1 teaspoon salt into a bowl, make a well in the centre and gradually work in the eggs, egg yolk, oil and enough water to form a soft dough.

2 Turn out on to a lightly floured surface and knead gently for 5 minutes until the dough is smooth and elastic. Brush with a little oil, cover and leave to rest for 30 minutes.

Makes sufficient for 4 servings

basic pizza dough

italy

There are several important factors to remember when making pizzas at home. First, always preheat a baking sheet to ensure the base of the pizza crisps as it cooks. Second, a pizza should have a really thin base, so roll the dough thinly before adding the topping of your choice. Third, a pizza must be eaten as soon as possible once it's cooked, so cook in batches rather than trying to cook more than one at a time.

1 Stir the yeast into the warm water until dissolved. Stir in 4 tablespoons of the flour and the sugar and leave in a warm place for 10 minutes, until really frothy.

2 Sift the remaining flour into a bowl, add the salt and make a well in the centre. Gradually work in the frothed yeast mixture and oil to form a soft dough, then knead for 8–10 minutes on a lightly floured surface.

3 Shape the dough into a ball and place in an oiled bowl. Cover with oiled plastic and leave to rise in a warm place for 1 hour, until doubled in size. Roll and use as required.

Makes two 35 cm (14 inch) bases or four 23 cm (9 inch) bases

1 teaspoon dry active yeast

150 ml (¼ pint) warm water

250 g (8 oz) strong white flour, plus extra for dusting

pinch of caster sugar

1 teaspoon sea salt

1 tablespoon extra virgin olive oil